the laws of
subtraction

the laws of
subtraction
matthew e. may

Six Simple Rules for Winning
in the Age of Excess Everything

NEW YORK   CHICAGO   SAN FRANCISCO
LISBON   LONDON   MADRID   MEXICO CITY   MILAN
NEW DELHI   SAN JUAN   SEOUL   SINGAPORE
SYDNEY   TORONTO

2 3 4 5 6 7 8 9 0   QFR/QFR   1 8 7 6 5 4 3 2

ISBN 978-0-07-179561-6
MHID   0-07-179561-8

e-ISBN 978-0-07-179562-3
e-MHID   0-07-179562-6

Design by Lee Fukui and Mauna Eichner

McGraw-Hill books are available at special quantity discounts to use as premiums and sales promotions or for use in corporate training programs. To contact a representative, please e-mail us at bulksales@mcgraw-hill.com.

This book is printed on acid-free paper.

Library of Congress Cataloging-in-Publication Data

May, Matthew E.
 The laws of subtraction : 6 simple rules for winning in the age of excess everything / Matthew May. — 1
    p. cm.
 Includes index.
 ISBN-13: 978-0-07-179561-6 (hardback)
 ISBN-10: 0-07-179561-8 ()
 1. Success in business. 2. Creative ability in business. 3. Simplicity. I. Title.
 HF5386.M4713 2012
 650.1—dc23
                                    2012027956

CONTENTS

GRATITUDE

One third of this book was not created by me but by over 50 amazingly gifted individuals who floored me with their willingness to contribute their inspiring thoughts about the theme of subtraction. Two days before Christmas 2011, I sent notes to six dozen or so individuals whose work I've admired and been inspired by. I invited them to be part of *The Laws of Subtraction* and share their thoughts. Knowing how busy they all were, I figured I might get one out of five to participate. I was giddy with shock when the enthusiastic acceptances came pouring in. By the time 2012 rolled around, nearly everyone had said yes. Obviously, this book would not be the same without you—your additions made subtraction worth reading about. Thank you, one and all!

Moe Abdou
Paul Akers
Teresa Amabile
Scott Belsky
Seth Berkowitz
Justin Brady
Brian Buck
Tanner Christensen
Chip Conley
Nancy Duarte
Jonathan Fields
Markus Flanagan
Jamie Flinchbaugh
Carmine Gallo
Bob Harrison
Sally Hogshead
John Hunter
Bill Jensen

Seth Kahan
Jonathan Kay
Dan Keldsen
Hal Macomber
John Maeda
Dan Markovitz
Karen Martin
Roger Martin
Kevin Meyer
Jon Miller
Robert Morris
Don Norman
Bernd Nürnberger
Nick Obolensky
Lisa Occhipinti
Shawn Parr
Mary Poppendieck
Diego Rodriguez

Bruce Rosenstein
Dan Schawbel
Jeffrey Schwartz
Tony Schwartz
Tina Seelig
Stephen Shapiro
David Sherwin
John Shook
Peter Sims
Derek Sivers
Brad Smith
Michael Bungay Stanier
Robert Sutton
William Taylor
Jeffrey Unger
Khoi Vinh
Helen Walters

And, of course, the anonymous artist(s) *PleaseFindThis*.

PROBLEM

EXCESS EVERYTHING

WHY SUBTRACTION?

To attain knowledge, add things every day.
To attain wisdom, subtract things every day.
Lao Tzu

I'm sure you have a story like this. In preparing for our annual family camping trip, I perform the obligatory equipment check. Of course, all the flashlights need new D-cell batteries. Off to the local hardware store I go, since we don't stockpile batteries in the refrigerator the way some folks do. When I return home, the fun begins. I'm not talking about the camping trip. I'm talking about trying to get the batteries open. The plastic packaging is super heavy-duty, slick and hard to grasp. It's deceiving, because it looks like it should easily pull apart. It doesn't, and for the life of me, I can't get the thing open. Feelings of inadequacy creep in: I must be missing something. It can't be this hard, can it? I begin blame shifting, wondering what possessed the package designers to think they needed this clearly excessive level of protection for a $6 purchase. A nearby package of lightbulbs—perhaps the most fragile household items on the planet, protected by nothing more than a flimsy bit of corrugated cardboard—is laughing at me. Frustration is mounting, as I've already wasted four minutes, and I need to open three of these. I grab the kitchen scissors and try to cut into the case, but the double-reinforced edge stops me cold. I need to somehow pierce the softer middle with something sharp. Steak knife to the rescue. I'm able to make a cut, not without a good bit of muscle, mind you, but I'm in. I try prying apart the opening, slicing my thumb on the razorsharp plastic edge I've created. I'm bleeding. That's when the cursing starts.

You can imagine the rest.

You're right to think this is a silly story about a benign annoyance. I tell it only to introduce in a lighthearted way a challenge far more serious and frustrating than trying to break open a package of batteries. It's the larger and more serious problem we all face: thriving in a world of excess everything.

The world is more overwhelming than ever before. Our work is deeper and more demanding than ever. Our businesses are more complicated and difficult to manage than ever. Our economy is more uncertain than ever. Our resources are scarcer than ever. There is endless choice and feature overkill in all but the best experiences. Everybody knows everything about us. The simple life is a thing of the past. Everywhere, there's too much of the wrong stuff and not enough of the right. The noise is deafening, the signal weak. Everything is too complicated and time-sucking. Excess everything is choking us.

Amazingly, as consumers, we seem to put up with it. We tolerate the intolerable: stupidly standing in some silly line, searching for what we want through the convoluted floor plan of the local mammoth warehouse store, or struggling through the maze of whatever automated voice mail system we're up against—or opening a package of D-cell batteries.

You'd think that if we hate all the excess as a consumer, we would absolutely detest it as a producer. But we don't. The reason we don't is that we see no clear and immediate path to turning things around. We know that the situation isn't going away. We know that we can't run or hide from it. So we shrug our shoulders and go along with the herd.

But.

At the heart of every difficult decision lie three tough choices: What to pursue versus what to ignore. What to leave in versus what to leave out. What to do versus what to don't. I have discovered that if you focus on the second half of each choice—what to ignore, what to leave out, what to don't—the decision becomes exponentially easier and simpler. The key is to remove the stupid stuff: anything obviously excessive, confusing, wasteful, unnatural, hazardous, hard to use, or ugly. (Battery packaging exhibits all seven qualities in a rather inglorious way.) Better yet, refrain from adding them in the first place.

This is the art of *subtraction*: when you remove just the right thing in just the right way, something good usually happens.

I believe subtraction is the path through the haze and maze, one that can allow us to create clarity from complexity and to wage and win the war against the common enemy of excess. And if that's so, if subtraction is the new skill to be gained, we need a guide to developing it. If subtraction is the new thinking, we need a fresh take on how to rethink everything we do. If subtraction is our weapon against excess everything, we need to know how to use it in battle.

That's not easy, because subtraction doesn't come naturally or intuitively—not to me, not to anyone. From the days of our ancestors on the savanna, we are hardwired to add and accumulate, hoard and store. This not only helps explain why the world is the way it is, it also lays out the real challenge: battling our instinct. We need to acknowledge and understand that to employ subtraction is to think differently. I mean that quite literally: neuroscientists have shown, using functional magnetic resonance imaging (fMRI), that addition and subtraction require different brain circuitry.

That's where *The Laws of Subtraction* comes in, drawing on this scientific fact to guide new and innovative thinking on how people can produce better results by artfully and intelligently using less. I cannot emphasize the word *better* enough. We hear a lot about doing more with less. You won't hear that from me. You will only hear about doing better with less. *Big* difference. There simply is no limit on better.

The Laws of Subtraction is meant to be a guide to creating more engaging *experiences* not only for others but also for ourselves. It is the experience that intrigues me, because whether it springs from a product, a process, a service, a project, a new business start-up, or a personal performance strategy, it is the experience that matters most. It is the experience that stays with us, and it is the experience that makes something meaningful. Focusing on the experience puts us in touch with the more emotional side of ideas. Understanding the human factors involved in producing an experience that fundamentally improves how we think, feel, or behave is what makes the design of any particular thing interesting.

The Laws of Subtraction is the book I've wanted to write for some time. I have broached the subject as a subtopic in my two previous books, first in *The Elegant Solution* and then in *In Pursuit of Elegance*, in which I devoted a chapter to subtraction as an element of elegance. I offer this final treatment on the power of less for two reasons.

Reason 1: Subtraction is what people want me to talk about in speeches and seminars. They ask me for rules of thumb to help them design and deliver more compelling experiences for themselves, their companies, and their customers. My friend and fellow author, the brilliant Daniel H. Pink, advised me not long ago at a corporate conference where we were both speaking just before he took the stage: "Subtraction is your meme," he told me. "It's out there; it's growing." He thought I should follow it and own it.

Best. Advice. Ever.

Reason 2: I am far from mastering subtraction, but for over a decade I've been a student of it: chasing down ideas of various kinds that are simple and powerful at the same time. My search began during my tenure as an advisor to Toyota; continued through an eight-year run during which I learned to appreciate the Japanese culture, the Eastern perspective, and how to "think lean"; and became most intense when I left that partnership in 2006 and launched myself into the world of public writing, speaking, and coaching. I was influenced greatly by the work of John Maeda, whose elegant book *The Laws of Simplicity* was published in the same year. In many respects, *The Laws of Subtraction* is an acknowledgment of the impact John Maeda's work has had on my own; beyond that, it picks up where his book left off: delving into and unraveling his tenth law: "Simplicity is about subtracting the obvious, and adding the meaningful."

I distill Maeda's tenth law into six simple rules:

1. What *isn't* there can often trump what *is*.

2. The simplest rules create the most effective experience.

3. Limiting information engages the imagination.

4. Creativity thrives under intelligent constraints.

5. *Break* is the important part of break*through*.

6. Doing something *isn't* always better than doing nothing.

I claim no credit for inventing these rules. They come from my search and research. In the last five years I've tracked down and examined over 2,000 ideas that to some degree fit a single criterion: they achieve maximum effect through minimum means. Those ideas span a wide spectrum of human endeavor: business, government, academia, arts, athletics, science, architecture, design, technology, and psychology. It is the common characteristics and recognizable patterns in these ideas that give rise to the six laws of subtraction, which when taken together can be thought of as a code for the creative mind.

I have organized the book around these six laws, devoting a single chapter to each one. I attempt to accomplish the two things I think a good book should do well: inform and inspire. I'll use a variety of methods to do so. In each chapter, I'll introduce you to a few illustrative examples of how a particular law was applied in a powerful way. I'll draw on both ancient Eastern philosophy and modern Western science wherever possible to help explain what goes on in our brains and offer some insight into why a certain law is so effective.

As for inspiration, I invited some of the most brilliant, noteworthy, and fascinating people I know to contribute their personal stories of subtraction and share with you how they embraced the power of less in their work and lives. There are over fifty stories, each one incredibly powerful and insightful, each one useful in helping you apply the laws of subtraction to your own work and life in ways I cannot. I've grouped them loosely according to the six laws, and they can be found after each chapter in the "Silhouettes in Subtraction" section.

I'm sure you realize the inherent contradiction at play in writing and publishing a book: it is an act of addition, not subtraction. If I could figure out how to get this particular portfolio of insight and inspiration into your head with an affordable form of magic that removes the written word entirely, I would. The best I can do is to follow John Maeda's guidance within my given constraint: subtract the obvious and add the meaningful.

My job in writing *The Laws of Subtraction* is both to challenge you and to help you to think a bit differently by using subtraction to do better with less and find clever solutions to your most difficult challenges, whatever they may be. If I do my job right, this book will have great meaning for you. If I don't, I'm sure you'll let me know.

I often ask other authors to tell me the one thing they would like their readers to take away from their books. For *The Laws of Subtraction*, it is quite simply this:

When you remove just the right things in just the right way, something good happens.

— Matthew E. May

LAW NO. 1

WHAT *ISN'T* THERE CAN

OFTEN TRUMP WHAT *IS*

Music is the space between the notes.
Claude Debussy

WHAT ISN'T THERE

love optical illusions. Here's why: The white circles that you see in the rather incomplete grid below don't really exist. Neither do the white diagonal lines you see connecting them. Yet what isn't really there is the most interesting part of the image.

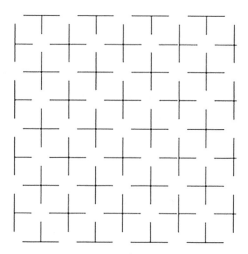

The reason it's so interesting isn't just that you see the white circles and diagonals, it's that *everyone* does. And even if I tell you to focus only on the drawn lines and completely ignore the space between them, your brain will override the order. So will everyone else's.

Harvard psychologist Daniel Gilbert refers to this as a mistake. "The errors that optical illusions induce in our perceptions are lawful, regular, and systematic," he says in his book *Stumbling on Happiness*. "They are not dumb mistakes but smart mistakes—mistakes that allow those who understand them to glimpse the elegant design and inner workings of the visual system."

It appears that I created the effect simply by removing a section of line segment on alternating corners of a larger grid composed of smaller squares. That's not quite accurate; it was a bit more involved than that. I experimented with the spacing of gaps to figure out the minimum amount of solid line needed to facilitate the production of an altogether new experience that *you*—or, more precisely, your brain—actually created.

You have just experienced the first law of subtraction: *What* isn't *there can often trump what* is.

If you know what to do and how to do it, you can use this approach to achieve success in the real world. You can cut through the noise and confusion of a chaotic world so that even the most complex things make more sense. You can draw and direct attention to what matters most so that your products and services have more meaning for others. You can focus energy and make your strategy more effective. You can generate greater visual and verbal impact to make your message stick and stay.

FedEx used Law 1 to dramatically change its image and create one of the most indelible logos ever designed, one that helped breathe new life into an already strong brand and simultaneously signaled the world that the company was going places.

Here's what happened.

HIDING IN PLAIN SIGHT

My 10-year-old daughter points out the logo on a FedEx truck every time she sees one. She's done that without fail ever since she learned to sound out letters. But she doesn't do that with any other logo. What's special about the FedEx logo isn't the vibrant colors or the bold lettering. It's the white arrow between the *E* and the *x*. "There's the white arrow that no one on my gymnastics team knows about," she'll say.

The FedEx logo is legendary among designers. It has won over 40 design awards and was ranked as one of the eight best logos in the last 35 years in the 35th Anniversary American Icon issue of *Rolling Stone* magazine. Nearly every design school professor and graphic designer with a blog has at some point focused on the FedEx logo to discuss the use of negative space. I wanted to hear the full history of how it all went down, not to mention impressing my daughter, so I called on Lindon Leader, the designer who created the mark in 1994 while working as senior design director in the San Francisco office of Landor Associates, a global brand consultancy known for executing strategy through design. Lindon now runs his own shop in Park City, Utah, where he continues to work the white space in creating marks and logos for a wide array of organizations.

We spoke at length about visual impact, his creative process, and his story of the FedEx logo development. I began by telling him how my daughter points out FedEx trucks when she sees them.

"It's those kinds of stories that are the most gratifying for me, most rewarding," he says. "I'm always asked what it's like to see your work everywhere, and does it ever get old. It never does."

When Lindon graduated from the Art Center College of Design in Pasadena, California, his very first job was with Saul Bass, the iconic Los Angeles designer perhaps best known for creating the AT&T logo. Lindon remembers Bass telling a story much like mine toward the end of his career. Someone asked him in an interview whether after an illustrious 40-year career in design in which he won every award under the sun, he still got a thrill out of design. Bass answered the question by explaining how he'd been driving recently with his five-year-old daughter, who suddenly cried out, "Daddy, look, there goes one of your trucks!" Saul told the interviewer that seeing that truck on the road still made him proud.

I shared my interest in subtraction, specifically the use of negative space and emptiness, and asked Lindon to describe his design philosophy. "I strive for two things in design: simplicity and clarity," he explains. "Great design is born of those two things. I think that's what we all want from design, and from business, from our work, even from our friendships."

According to Lindon, seeing the original Smith & Hawken catalogs in the 1980s made a significant impression on him and influenced much of his early approach to design. "It was an experience like taking this leisurely stroll through a garden, everything so clean, refreshing, uncluttered. You got this sense of the simple, healthy outdoors life. Simple and clear. It was my first aha into what design needs to be."

Lindon begins a design project in a fairly typical way, generating a long string of designs. "Those early sketches always have too much going on, too much to think about, and too much extraneous stuff," he says. He labors over the work until the simplicity and clarity he's looking for begin to emerge. "I slowly begin to remove things. The more you pull out, the clearer it gets. Not everyone gets that; most people don't. But it's always the final one that's far more simple and far more clear than the more elaborate ones I labored over at the beginning." It is inevitable, he says, that when he creates something composed of 30 to 40 percent whitespace, his clients ask why they can't fill up the space and make use of it. Lindon's invariable reply: "Understatement is much more effective, much more elegant."

Elaborating on the theme of understatement and how to craft a memorable experience through something as apparently limiting as graphic identity design, Lindon explains to me that what he's after is what he calls "the punch line" and that he's delighted when something isn't what it appears to be at first glance: "You look at something, then you look at it again, and you say, 'Hey, wait!' and 'Oh, I get it!'" Lindon is after what he refers to as "one plus one equals three." For Lindon, that addition is actually subtractive. "You've eliminated the third one and had not just the same impact but greater impact because of the surprise of the missing one. If your name is Global Air Supply, for example, the last thing you want is an airplane flying around an image of the globe. That's one plus one equals two. The FedEx logo without the hidden arrow is just plain vanilla—one plus one equals two. *With* it, it's one plus one equals three."

"If you look at the original Northwest Orient Airlines logo that Landor Associates did," Lindon continues, "it's maybe the best logo I've ever seen. It's one plus one equals three, maybe four or five." The logo he is referring to is shown on the next page. It is a circle with a clearly visible *N*. But if you look again, you see it's also a *W*: part of the left leg of the *W* is removed. And it's even more than that: the circle represents the compass, and the whitespace simultaneously creates a little tick, a pointer, pointing northwest.

"It's pure genius," states Lindon. "The old Bank of America logo, too, is one of my favorites." That logo, shown on the next page, reveals that the *B* and the *A* are created with whitespace. That space, if you look at it, is in the shape of an American eagle. "Brilliant," he confirms. "Negative space, white space, it's incredibly important. There's a reason the Apple logo is now whitespace. It says plenty about the simple design and functionality of

their products. But it's even more than that; it says 'our products speak for themselves.' It's bold, shows confidence. It's not just a graphic element; it's a fully realized identity."

It was that kind of artistry that Lindon was after in developing the FedEx logo. "Back then, the company was still officially Federal Express," he recalls. "The logo was a purple and orange wordmark that simply spelled out the name. By the way, people in focus groups thought it was blue and red, but it wasn't. It had this incredible customer-created brand. Everyone said 'FedEx' and used it as a verb." Although there was enormous cachet around the term, a global research study revealed that customers were unaware of Federal Express's global scope and full-service logistics capabilities.

"People thought they shipped only overnight and only within the U.S.," Lindon explains. "So the goal was to communicate the breadth of its services and to leverage one of its most valuable assets—the FedEx brand." Lindon remembers that FedEx's CEO, Fred Smith, placed high value on design and had an intuitive marketing sense: "Any designer worth a lick will tell you great clients make for great design. He said okay to a brand name change and authorized a new graphic treatment. He said do whatever we wanted, under two conditions. One was that whatever we did, we had to justify it: 'You can make them pink and green for all I care; just give me a good reason why,' he said. The second one was about visibility. 'My trucks are moving billboards,' he said. 'I better be able to see a FedEx truck loud and clear from five blocks away.' That was it! So off we went."

I asked Lindon to take me through the design process in as much step-by-step detail as he could remember. "We had two or three teams working on it," he begins. "We developed about 200 design concepts, everything from evolutionary to revolutionary. It was a full spectrum. We knew we had to respect the brand cachet but extract the real value, make key decisions on what to keep, what to delete, what was usable, and what wasn't. For example, we knew we wanted to keep the orange and purple—it was recognizable, so we wanted to exploit that—but make the orange less red and the purple less blue."

At the time, Lindon was "in love with two bold fonts" known as Univers 67, which is a condensed bold type, and Futura Bold. He takes me through how he started playing with the two typefaces and the letter spacing, from extremely wide to locked together, uppercase and lowercase, mixing and tinkering. One iteration had a capital *E* and a lowercase *x*: "I started squeezing the letter spacing, I saw a white arrow start to appear between the *E* and the *x*. I thought, 'There's something there.' I tried both fonts, but I didn't like how much I had to distort either typeface to make the arrow look good. I thought, 'Would it be possible to blend the best features of both?' I took the high *x* of Univers and mixed it with the stroke of Futura Bold. The *x* rose to the crossbar of a lowered *E*. I kept tweaking, and eventually not only did the arrow look natural and unforced, but I ended up with a whole new letterform."

A handful of the other designs contained arrows, but none were hidden. "I thought, 'Okay, there's nothing really compelling about an arrow,'" Lindon remembers. "It's overused and rather mundane. But I thought we could build a story around it." The arrow could connote forward direction, speed, and precision, and if it remained hidden, there might be an element of surprise, that aha moment. "I didn't overplay it, didn't mention it. And you know, most of our own designers didn't see it! But when I previewed the mark along with a few others with the global brand manager, she asked, 'Is there an arrow in there?' She saw it, and it was game on!"

I wanted to know more about that aha moment when people got the punch line. I could hear the smile in his voice: "I remember it like it was yesterday." On April 23, 1994, the Landor team presented their design ideas at FedEx headquarters in Memphis, Tennessee. The hidden arrow mark was one of five presented to a fairly large group of senior executives. "We had built prototypes of planes, vans, and trucks. We would never just show designs on paper unless that was the only application. You need the context. We presented the whole of our work with no mention of the hidden arrow. Our goal was to not reveal it, to see if it got discovered. The global brand manager knew, of course, but kept the secret. Amazingly, Fred Smith was the only one to see the arrow right away. It's probably why it won. Once everyone saw it, once they got the punch line, they loved it."

According to Lindon, there's always a temptation and tendency to go overboard and start adding and complicating matters, which indeed happened with FedEx. "People aren't good at restraint," he says. "They don't get that not adding is really a form of subtracting. All of a sudden there was this rush to tell the world the secret. Sort of defeats the purpose, don't you think? FedEx's PR firm immediately wanted to supersize it. They wanted to make it obvious, fill it in with another color. They wanted to feature the arrow in other brand communications. They didn't get it. It wasn't about the arrow. An arrow isn't even interesting to look at. It's only because of the subtlety that it's intriguing. And not seeing the arrow doesn't in any way detract from the power of the mark. The arrow's just an added, novel bonus. We said no way. I tell people this all the time. Henny Youngman, the comedian, had this whole signature to his act around 'Take my wife. Please.' What the PR folks wanted to do was the equivalent of changing his shtick to 'Please, take my wife.' If you have to call attention to your punch line, to explain it, it's no longer a punch line. It doesn't work, it isn't funny, and no one will remember it."

Lindon Leader's design is considered by many to be one of the most creative logos ever designed. Not because of what's there but because of what isn't.

WHAT ISN'T THERE

I spend about 10 hours a week riding a bike, which is nothing compared with the 40 that professional cyclists spend in the saddle. Still, that's a lot of contact with the bicycle seat, and it's the universal source of several physical maladies afflicting avid cyclists, ranging from numbness, to saddle sores, to prostate problems, to impotency. It's no wonder that as *Bicycling* magazine's former chief technical editor Jim Langley quips on his "Bicycle Aficionado" site, "Few products in the history of sports have taken such a bum rap."

It's taken over 150 years for bike saddles to evolve to the sleek designs used today. Until recently, the evolution focused on addition: more cushion, more shock absorption, more surface area—all in the name of elusive comfort.

One company centers its entire operation on the bicycle seat: Selle Italia, situated in Casella d'Asolo, outside Venice, Italy. Making saddles by hand that provide maximum performance and comfort has been Selle Italia's sole focus since the company was established in 1897.

The saddle pictured here is mine. It's a lifesaver. The product description for the $300 seat reads: "The Selle Italia SLR SuperFlow Saddle is remarkable for the amount of saddle real estate that's missing. Not to worry, it's all part of the design." The original design was introduced in 1998 with the Trans Am saddle, which featured a 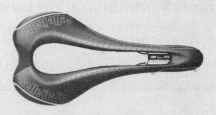 slim opening in the seat middle to relieve pressure. Over time, weight and material have been removed through constant research and innovation.

When Giuseppe Bigolin, the president of Selle Italia, explained the company's narrow focus to me, he talked in terms of innovation.

"One strong and clear word says everything about us," he wrote. "Innovation. It's our past, our present, and our future. No ideas from our laboratories are ever discarded. We don't cancel a project if it is too difficult to do."

The anatomic cutout is only one of several subtractive strategies Selle Italia employs in its design. Carbon fiber technology is used throughout the product line to reduce weight while increasing structural strength and durability. A special comolding process uses a patented elastomer to allow a flexible suspension system that eliminates road shock and vibration without the use of heavy, noisy springs while achieving a 40 percent reduction of weight without any loss of comfort. It was Selle Italia that in 1984 first patented the use of silicone gel as the primary padding element, an innovation that not only saves weight but is more durable and absorbs 40 percent more shock than standard gels and 350 percent more than traditional foam padding.

Selle Italia continues to raise the standard in bicycle performance and aesthetics and has turned the saddle from a mere component of the bicycle into a factor of well-being for the rider, ultimately making it a cult object for athletes.

"Innovate or remain faithful to tradition?" asks Bigolin. "Both. We have been carrying out this activity for over a hundred years, perfecting it, interpreting saddle needs over the decades."

Selle Italia will undoubtedly be doing just that for another hundred years. Its strategy is almost entirely one of subtraction.

THE GESTALT OF DESIGN

The gestalt theory of perception holds that people tend to see related parts as a unified whole rather than a simple sum of the parts when certain principles of perception are applied. The gestalt principles help describe the visual effects of designs such as the FedEx logo.

The group of principles most closely related to subtraction falls under what's known as the *law of prägnanz*, German for "pregnant," as in pregnant with meaning. The law holds that we tend to perceive ambiguous, uncertain, incomplete, and complex things in their simplest and most complete form.

In designing the FedEx logo, Lindon Leader invoked the law of prägnanz principle known as figure–ground. The reason you're able to read this book is that black *figures* on a white back*ground* are the easiest to read. Designer Andy Rutledge uses extremely simple examples such as the one shown here to quickly illustrate the principle. The images you see appear to be different, yet they have identical composition. The image on the left shows a gray figure resting on a white background. The one on the right is perceived as a gray figure with a hole in it. Both are placed on a white background.

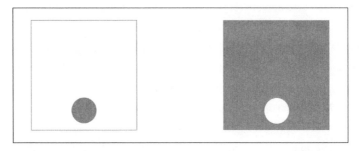

In reality, all these perceptions are mistakes—smart mistakes, though, that give meaning to the objects and their relationship to one another. As Andy says: "These relationships are determined both by contrast and by common conventions of human experience."

The gestalt principles are merely descriptive classifications of visual perception and don't provide an explanation of how and why our brains perform the way they do. Yet even neuroscience is at this point unable to provide a precise explanation, at least of the why. The best explanation may be related to evolution. According to James Wise, a Washington State University associate professor of environmental psychology, our earliest ancestors on the African plains could detect the subtle difference between tall grass that was swayed by the wind and grass that was disturbed by a predator. In other words, to survive in the savanna, the human brain developed into a terrific pattern-recognizing, pattern-making machine. The ability to use patterns to create meaningful relationships from seemingly unrelated elements is a uniquely human attribute and the hallmark of creativity.

What really matters in all this is to be aware that these principles of perception exist and to be able to use them the way Lindon Leader did in creating the FedEx logo. We need to pay attention to the fact that what isn't there can often trump what is.

The first law of subtraction can also be applied in a less literal, more conceptual yet strategic way to create an end-to-end experience.

SELLING EMPTY SPACE

On a sunny Saturday afternoon late in 2011, a crowd of grindcore music lovers lined up outside The Roxy on Sunset Boulevard in West Hollywood, California, to get free T-shirts—not of Repulsion, the band that was playing there, but of the Scion xB. You've seen a Scion xB on the road: those little boxy numbers that look like a 1950s milk truck that got together with a toaster and made babies. If not, here's a picture of the original 2003 model.

Image courtesy of Scion.

Who'd want to drive such a thing? My thought exactly when I got a peek at it before the March 2002 debut at the New York International Auto Show. It turns out that I was just showing my advanced age, because Generation Y, the so-called New Millennials, the generation born between 1980 and 1994, scooped them up as quickly as they hit showroom floors in June 2003.

The almost overnight success hinged on what was left out of the traditional marketing approach.

Success Is an Option

In the late 1990s, Toyota had to face the reality that by 2020, the 60 million New Millennials would constitute 40 percent of the U.S. new-car market. The average 50-plus-year-old Toyota customer was going to be replaced by a twentysomething buyer who was everything the current buyer wasn't: brand-sensitive, superinformed, ethnically diverse, difficult to reach, technologically savvy, well connected, luxury-oriented, discriminating, and demanding with a significant disposable income and strong sense of entitlement, seeking fun and entertainment.

I watched Toyota's first attempt fail. A special team called Genesis was formed in 1999 to craft a new marketing strategy, using a model called the Echo, a reference to members of Gen Y known as echo boomers, children of baby boomers, born in the 1980s. Marketing centered on Internet and cable television commercials, special retail showroom displays, and sponsorship of extreme sports competition and concert events. The effort dropped the average age of Echo buyers all of five years, from 43 to 38.

Gen Y had seen through the strategy. It didn't much matter how slick or "alternative" the marketing was; they simply weren't going to buy a brand that Mom and Dad owned. No self-respecting New Millennial wanted to be caught dead in a car known for quality, durability, and reliability. Echo had no verve or edge, wasn't in any way distinct or unique, and had nothing to offer Gen Y. Genesis missed the fact that the younger generation was allergic to any kind of advertising in the first place.

The experiment lasted less than two years. Toyota went back to the drawing board, knowing it needed a new kind of car and a new kind of experience specifically developed for this new kind of buyer.

The solution was Scion.

Observe First, Design Second

Step one for Toyota developers was a practice known as *genchi genbutsu* (gen-chee-gen-BOOT-soo), Japanese for "go look, go see." The practice is simple: observe first, design second. It's essentially a gathering phase.

Designers have their own term for this: *empathizing*. The goal is to observe people and their behavior in the context of their entire lives. Empathizing is the initial step in a good design process, and it's a valuable skill for everyone to develop regardless of profession.

Roger Martin, dean of the University of Toronto's innovative Rotman School of Management and author of several books on "design thinking," argues, "Businesspeople don't just need to understand designers; they need to *be* designers." He's right. It's tough to create a compelling solution unless you thoroughly understand the problem your customer or user is trying to solve, which every mortal designer worth a lick aims to do by first immersing himself or herself in the world of those with the problem.

Yet it's the very step that Genesis bypassed, which is curious because *genchi genbutsu* is part of the Toyota DNA. It also figured centrally in the design and launch in the late 1980s of Toyota's luxury brand, Lexus.*

With Scion, the *genchi genbutsu* focused on attending raves, concerts of the most popular bands and musicians, extreme sporting events, and urban street art shows—all the places and spaces where Gen Y hung out. I spoke with Kevin Hunter, who heads CALTY Design Research, Toyota's California design center, to get his take on the process.

"People can't tell you what they want in the future," Kevin says. "And they often don't even know what they want now. So you can't just ask them, because they can't or won't tell you in a way that's helpful. They often don't know what they really need. They often can't articulate it well. You have to discover to uncover the need. You do that not just by watching and interviewing them but by becoming them, infiltrating them almost like an undercover cop, and then involving them in the design."

That's just what the Scion team did. And as with the Lexus project, the *genchi genbutsu* gave it great insight into the new generation of car buyers.

In the mid-1980s, the design team responsible for Toyota's secret luxury concept holed up in a luxury beachfront home in Laguna Beach, California, and lived the affluent lifestyle in Los Angeles for months to better understand upscale buyers. The experience proved invaluable in the ability of Lexus to instantly topple Mercedes-Benz and BMW models in Car and Driver *reviews. I will tell the full story in Chapter 3 from the perspective of how constraints drive creativity and innovation.*

Speak Unique

The team discovered that personal expression was the most powerful motivation for Gen Y. If something couldn't be altered, customized, tailored, or in some way personalized to make a statement of individuality, they weren't much interested. It wasn't about the things they owned, it was about what they could *do* to them. The team also learned why advertising was frowned upon: Gen Y didn't like being told what to like or buy, didn't like being pushed. *Discovering* something new, cool, and different was part of their joy.

That insight explained why Genesis failed and formed the basis for a new strategy: overhaul the entire Scion experience to reflect the Gen Y attitude. Everything about Scion had to be completely, radically rethought to evoke a single word in the mind of the buyer: *unique.*

First came the car, which was based on an unusually simple and spare concept car designed in Japan called the bB. The bB featured unusual styling, yet it was versatile and fun to drive. The name was updated to xB, to play up the "extreme" nature of the car. Dozens of feature specifications standard on other Toyota vehicles were removed. The number of options and accessories was tripled: Toyota models averaged 15 options; Scion offered over 40. The combination of spartan specifications and a wide array of options and accessories was paired with online configuration (check out scionxpressionism.com). The entire car was designed so that buyers could add their signatures and make an xB uniquely their own.

Scion set the price bar low: not only was the $15,000 purchase price set at rock bottom, so were the retail margins. The dealer margin for the Scion was set at 6 percent, about half the Toyota figure. Scion employed something they called *pure pricing*: dealers set their own retail prices, publicized those prices, and then stuck to them. The goal was to simplify the purchasing process and eliminate the biggest sources of Gen Y's headache: price ambiguity and aggressive negotiation. The pricing of Scion vehicles would be transparent, simple, and consistent.

One reason U.S. automobile dealers haggle over price is the inability to match supply with demand. If the perfect vehicle is unavailable, dealers will push hard on the customer to buy the car that's in stock. It's a painful experience, and most people would rather go to the dentist than visit a car dealership.

Scion management decided to remove that pain and gave dealers an edict in the form of a written covenant: move from *push* to a *pull* or you don't get to be a Scion dealer. Under a pull system, Scion would market vehicle customization to customers—and dealers would accessorize vehicles—only upon a customer's specific request. The customer would pull a Scion vehicle through the system, much the way a Toyota factory assembly line works.

But that meant that customers might have to wait a week for the perfect Scion. That was fine, because the research had shown that Gen Y was prepared to wait for the right thing. Overall speed of purchasing actually shrank, because by the time most customers actually set foot inside the Scion corner, they had already configured and priced their custom cars on the Internet. If they hadn't, there was a distinct showroom zone where they could complete the process in a self-directed way.

The Genesis project taught Scion to avoid traditional advertising and instead favor low budgets with creative use of alternative channels, such as YouTube, cell phone videos, and *DUB* magazine articles featuring Scion cars getting pimped out. Live events took center stage: Scion both sponsored them and used them as live product displays. It was normal to see an xB adorned with banners reading "No Clone Zone" and "Ban Normality" in the middle of the venue grounds for people to discover on their own.

Music was and continues to be a key focus of Scion marketing. Scion began by sponsoring concerts but soon moved into funding independent bands and artists. Scion was one of the first national brands in the United States to buy into online radio, starting in 2005. Since then they've grown their presence in a number of unique ways. In 2008, Scion launched its own branded multichannel online radio station, Scion Radio 17.

A year later, they released a mobile app for iPhone, iTouch, and iPad called Scion Radio 17 BPM, which DJs love. The app automatically calculates the beats per minute (BPM) of a song as you tap the screen to the song's rhythm. After recording the song's BPM, you can create playlists by genre and send song lists with corresponding BPM information to yourself and others. DJs use it to plan live sets and recorded mixes. The app also provides a scrolling news ticker that keeps you up to date with the current month's Scion Radio 17 features.

Scion isn't selling cars. And rather than pushing glitzy advertising on its customers, Scion provides content that engages them with something they care about: music. Along the way marketers gain deeper insights into what makes their customers tick. According to Jeri Yoshizu, Scion's national sales promotion manager (and as of this writing the only member of the current Scion team who was there at the start in 2003), the whole idea is "to build goodwill through many small actions rather than a few large ones. Scion is always looking for ways to keep its customers engaged with the brand." The beauty of the strategy is how Scion marketers have been able to do that in a deceptively simple way that has little to do with the tangible good they make and sell. Scion recently announced that it is going to launch an independent recording label, a project called Scion A/V.

The Scion launch strategy scored a bull's-eye with Gen Y. It became Toyota's fastest-selling brand soon after launch, with nearly 90 percent of Scion buyers being new to Toyota. Cumulative sales topped 100,000 in less than 18 months. In late 2004, the xB received a bronze in the Industrial Design Excellence Awards, and Edmunds.com named the xB "the Most Wanted Wagon Under $15,000."

Near my home in southern California there is an empty dirt lot where on any given Saturday back in 2004 I would see a dozen xBs lined up in an ad hoc auto show. All the hatchbacks were open to display custom jobs: carbon fiber interiors, sound systems with subwoofers strong enough to rock a house, and flat screen TVs equipped with DVD machines. Kids put an average of $15,000 worth of aftermarket accessories into a $15,000 product. No one was looking at the car. They were looking at what was *done* to it. That's because Scion has never been about the car.

It's about what was left out of it.

THE ZEN OF NOTHING

During my time with Toyota, I became interested in Eastern culture. I had to, really, because much of my job consisted of designing programs that incorporated the views of both Japanese and U.S. management. Eastern and Western ways of looking at the world are often quite different and often diametrically opposed. Reconciling that tension in a harmonious way meant I had to understand the Asian perspective, which necessitated understanding the genesis of certain methods. I traced several to twelfth-century Zen philosophy, but Zen had its beginnings in far more ancient Chinese Taoism, which dates back several hundred years BC.

What struck me was the reverence given to emptiness as an aesthetic ideal. As I dug deeper into history, it became apparent that as Zen Buddhism took hold in Japan during the twelfth and thirteenth centuries, all facets of life and culture began to reflect the theme of emptiness, from art and architecture to commerce and community. In the Zen view, emptiness is a symbol of inexhaustible spirit. Silence in music and film, pauses in theater and dance, and blank spaces in paintings take on a special significance because it is in states of temporary inactivity or quietude that Zen practitioners see the very essence of creative energy.

Further, because in Zen the human spirit is thought to be indefinable, the power of suggestion is exalted as the mark of high creativity. Finiteness is at odds with nature, so the thought goes, which implies stagnation, which in turn is associated with loss of life. The goal of the Zen artist is to convey the perfect harmony of nature through clearly imperfect renderings; the result is that those viewing the art supply the missing symmetry and thus participate in the act of creation.

The renowned poet Fujiwara no Teika maintained that "the poet who has begun a thought must be able to end it so masterfully that a rich space of suggestions unfolds in the imagination of his audience." Teika's work became a guiding force in the development of Zen thought in Japan, and historians view his treatises on aesthetics as the equivalent of universal handbooks on the philosophy of art.

One of my favorite Zen-related words in Japanese is *ma*, not because it's one of the few I can pronounce correctly but because of what it means and what it doesn't. The rough translation is "interval of space or time." But that doesn't quite capture the essence, and no English words or concepts exist to accurately define or describe it. For me, it means being fully aware of what is and isn't there, being conscious of how they work together to involve the viewer in an altogether new experience, and understanding that to ignore either is to miss the true meaning of the whole.

Here is Isao Tsujimoto, former director general of the Japan Foundation in New York, speaking on the concept of *ma* in Japanese life and culture during the JapanNYC festival featuring Japanese Noh dance and theater at Carnegie Hall, dedicated to victims of the 2011 earthquake and tsunami in Japan:

> There is a concept called *ma*. *Ma* means empty . . . or distance . . . or blank . . . blankness. So if you see Japanese Noh theater, with Japanese music, there is plenty of *ma*, plenty of silence. Even in daily conversation, in Japanese, there is lots of *ma*. I always sense a difference between that kind of sense of time . . . of the Japanese . . . and Westerners. Especially Americans. In a conversation with American people, you need to keep talking. So I think the people have a kind of a fear . . . are a little afraid of having *ma* between my talk and your talk. But somehow Japanese people have a sense to enjoy that kind of blankness. That kind of notion reflects in every aspect of Japanese, especially traditional culture.

According to a course on Japanese history taught at Columbia University, "*Ma* is not something that is created by compositional elements; it is the thing that takes place in the imagination of the human who experiences these elements."

And *that* is the whole point of the first law of subtraction.

SILHOUETTES

IN SUBTRACTION

John Maeda

Roger Martin

Chip Conley

Bernd Nürnberger

Robert Sutton and Diego Rodriguez

Nancy Duarte

Scott Belsky

Stephen Shapiro

Jon Miller

PRIORITY OR FOCUS?

John Maeda

 As a designer I was trained to focus, to create with superhuman power, which is different from prioritizing. I wasn't trained to prioritize. Most designers aren't. Prioritization is a conscious act of stepping back and choosing what to remove from a long list of things you could do, which is different from focusing and executing down one path.

When I was a college professor and designer, I could focus on one particular area. As a college president, though, I'm facing a much broader set of questions and a different set of constraints. The difference between the two roles is an order of magnitude. It's like going from making something out of wood to making something out of the Internet. You go from something you can shape and control to a system that you can't possibly control. And in that, simplicity becomes about how to make a difference, and you can make a difference only if you prioritize.

Originally when I became president, I was using the technique I'd learned, which is focus, which works when you're trying to make something. But when you're trying to lead an institution, people don't really care about your focus except to the extent that attention is focused on what you prioritize. Everything I knew as a designer didn't apply to the new role.

Now, you might say that difference is just a nuance, like the difference between a ballpoint pen and a gel pen, for instance. But it was something I wasn't aware of. I had to learn, and I'm still learning.

I'm learning, for example, to turn off some of my creative instincts. Because when you think about it, prioritization is the opposite of creativity. Reduction is the opposite of creativity, which is about expanding the possibilities. It's divergent, whereas subtraction is about convergence. Creativity under the laws of subtraction is more complex, more about resourcefulness. But that's the essential difference, I think, between focus and prioritization.

I've learned to reduce my creative instincts around certain things when they're not producing results, which is hard because creative people believe in possibility, that a new approach will produce the result. When you're designing, subtraction is just one of those beautiful words. It's a Steve Jobs word. As a maker and creator, you can subtract anything you want. It's powerful.

When I think about the tenth law of simplicity, about subtraction, I'm able to see now after a few years of running a complex organization—a university—that there's an important difference between prioritization and focus. That leap was some leap to make.

John Maeda (@johnmaeda) is president of the Rhode Island School of Design and the author of The Laws of Simplicity.

SLICE IT THIN

Roger Martin

I think about my life as a series of pyramids. Each one is a project—à la "running Rotman" or "writing books" or "being on a board of directors"—in which the tasks can be stratified from most complex, enigmatic, and abstract to least. Because there are successively more of the latter as you go down from the peak, it is a pyramid rather than a cylinder.

Jobs are structured as slices of the pyramid, with more senior people being given slices higher up the pyramid. However, in my experience most jobs are doled out in slices that are far too thick, and the thickness is accepted without question by the recipient of the job.

This was evident to me when I was handed the thick bundle called "Dean of the Rotman School of Management." I immediately went to work thinning out my "running Rotman" pyramid. I had a very thick slice of budgeting, financial planning, and financial control.

This thin slicing gave me two wins.

First, it increased everyone's satisfaction. Second, it enabled me to take on additional pyramids such as writing articles and books that enhance our school's reputation.

People ask whether I get any sleep when they see all the activities I'm engaged in. I answer that I love sleep and get plenty of it. They assume I'm taking a thick slice of everything I do. I'm not. I relentlessly thin down.

Why don't more people do this? I think it's because most are unwilling to make the time-consuming design investment up front. If I would have simply tossed a bunch of financial responsibilities to my chief administrative officer and wished her the best of luck, it wouldn't have been a happy ending. I needed to work with her to make sure that we shared a similar view of what we were trying to accomplish.

Work is fun and productive when we're doing what we do best while those around us are doing what they do best. It's not so much fun when we're doing work that others are better at but aren't doing because we've failed to design the work properly.

I highly recommend thin slicing. Those I work with are happier and more productive because of it. As am I!

Roger Martin (rogermartin.com) is dean of the Rotman School of Management and the coauthor of Playing to Win: How Strategy Really Works. *In 2011 he placed sixth on the Thinkers50 list, a biannual ranking of the most influential global business thinkers.*

THE WISDOM EQUATION

Chip Conley

The beauty of wisdom is its simplicity.

Though we tend to think that wisdom is reserved for aging philosophers or, hopefully, your best friend when you're in an emotional jam, Aristotle believed that practical wisdom was available to all of us and that it was the master virtue for individuals and society.

I've come to realize that wisdom is fundamentally a subtractive virtue, not an additive one. Wise men filter insights when others get lost in piles and piles of knowledge.

T. S. Eliot wrote, "Where is the wisdom we have lost in knowledge? Where is the knowledge we have lost in information?" He wrote that long before we commonly referred to ours as an age of information overload.

Wisdom is all about distilling down the complexity of life, with all its distractions, to what's at its core. That's true in both our personal and our work lives. Your company doesn't become a customer service laggard because of a single customer service error with an important client. It is the series of repeated actions or issues that remain unresolved that creates a pattern of behavior and thinking that leads to a weakening service culture. That's why we hire consultants and coaches; they aren't necessarily any wiser than we are, but they're more objective in seeing the patterns.

The one quality that most consistently shows up in researchers' observations on wisdom is experience. That's why we consider those who have a few decades under their belts more likely to be wise than younger people. Life experience is the result of thousands or millions of tiny actions, each of which contributes to the larger whole. But wisdom seeks the core truth at the center.

What if the equation for wisdom is wisdom equals the square root of experience?

Our equation for life is one long series of additions. But the wisdom equation suggests quite the opposite: when we're faced with the greatest odds against us, often we need to edit rather than add.

If we are wise enough to contemplate our own experiences, we can figure out the square root—what's at the core—so that we can be not only wise but also heroic in using wisdom to take the right action to make fundamental changes in our lives.

In a world awash in quick fixes, lowest-common-denominator thinking, and the pursuit of efficiency, wisdom is our sanctuary of sanity. Wisdom is the ultimate editor of our lives. It sees the wheat and discards the chaff.

The magic of life is not in computing more but in learning to make sense with less.

Chip Conley (chipconley.com) is the cofounder and CEO of Joie de Vivre Hospitality and the author most recently of Emotional Equations, *from which he adapted this story.*

LEFT UNSAID

Bernd Nürnberger

From age 16 in Germany, I dreamed of working in the United States. I graduated from university and after a while got an 18-month contract as a domestic safety inspector for an electric/electronics equipment company based in the United States. When the contract was up, they asked me if I could go to Japan for six months and help out there. Two colleagues said, "You will not come back." Of course I will come back, I said; my dream is to work in the United States.

So I went to Japan. And I did not come back.

I had been there only two months. I spoke no Japanese, but I could do business in Japan because it was export-oriented, so English was spoken, which I spoke well. I was on a business trip with a Japanese colleague, and on our way back, we took a little sightseeing trip by taxi.

I noticed how he talked to the taxi driver. Not understanding a single word of Japanese, I thought, "Now this sounds very friendly." So I asked my colleague, "Do you know this taxi driver?" He said, "No, why?" "Well, because," I said, "this way of talking sounds really friendly to me." "That is how we always talk in Japan," he said.

I realized I had heard this way of talking, this tone of voice, many times before in those two months at restaurants, in shops, and so forth. I could not understand the words, but I could follow the conversation—not from what was spoken but from what wasn't—the tone, the mannerisms, and how it felt. At that moment it dawned on me that this was simply how people treated each other here. So I decided to stay.

Because I could not follow the language, that left room to perceive other things. The element of subtraction led to my keystone realization that this way of treating others is normal here, and I like it, and this is the place I want to be. A whole set of disconnected observations fell into place at that moment. I could put prior observations in alignment, and they now made sense to me.

I made an emotional decision, a *life* decision, based on what was not said in that taxi that day. That was 1986.

And I have been here ever since.

Bernd Nürnberger inspired the United Nations Global Compact efforts for TÜV Rheinland Group in Yokohama, Japan, and blogs at cocreatr.typepad.com.

GROUP SUBTRACTION

Robert Sutton and Diego Rodriguez

We've taught, consulted on, and carried out the various flavors of creativity, innovation, and design thinking for many years. We know dozens of people who are adept at guiding creative teams and boldly include ourselves as being among them. But Perry Klebahn stands alone as one of the very best.

Perry heads executive education at Stanford's Hasso Plattner Institute of Design, aka "the d.school." Those of us who've seen him in action are fans and, truth be told, secretly a bit envious of his ability. Perry has something truly special. He does so many important little things that it's impossible to describe all the tricks in his bag of magic. He is adept at keeping creative teams on track, helping those which are struggling, and, with remarkable frequency, saving teams that are flaming out, flailing, and seemingly unsalvageable.

Subtraction is a big part of Perry's tool kit.

Perry's magic is especially evident in what he does when creative teams are stuck. One move he makes early and often is to carefully neutralize especially destructive members. When people fuel destructive conflict, put down others' ideas without offering constructive alternatives, or play with their iPhones, he'll give them individual tasks or put all the bad apples in one group and even send them packing if it's feasible.

What's most interesting and instructive, though, is how well Perry's methods fit evidence on group effectiveness. Psychologist Roy Baumeister has shown that "bad is stronger than good" and that negative people do all sorts of damage to others: distracting them, upsetting them, and infecting them with the rotten apple's destructive behavior and attitudes. Researcher Will Phelps has shown that having just one bad apple in a small group can drag down performance by up to 40 percent. Richard Hackman of Harvard has shown that smaller teams are more effective than larger teams because as group size grows, more attention is devoted to running the group and less to the task at hand, and difficult group members place an especially heavy load on fellow group members.

We could go on about the ways Perry uses subtraction, including his efficiency of language—*Yep. Nope. Got it. I'll fix that*—and his all-time favorite: *Done.*

Perry's skill at removing unnecessary and destructive things helps explain why he is one of the best creative coaches we've ever seen.

Robert Sutton (bobsutton.net) is a professor of management science and engineering at Stanford and the author of The No Asshole Rule *and* Good Boss, Bad Boss. *Diego Rodriguez (metacool.type-pad.com) is a partner at IDEO and an associate consulting professor at the Stanford d.school.*

THE POWER OF NO

Nancy Duarte

When opportunity knocks, it's easy to open the door. It's harder to shut doors that flow with cash. But for my firm, saying no has been the key to our success.

We started up intending to be a small design firm. We became specialists in designing presentations almost by default: no one else wanted the work.

It was hard to find great designers to work on presentations because the design community hated the medium. The tools weren't sophisticated enough, and, unlike other design work, clients can change it any way they want. Designers don't like that.

At first I was embarrassed to tell people we designed slides. Even though I loved that we created presentations, people would look at me with pity in their voice and say, "I am so sorry." That only fueled my desire to be acknowledged as a *real* design firm.

During the dot-com boom, we took on web and print design. Our presentation design became a third thought. Business boomed at the same speed as the economy. We were winning great corporate identity projects and building beautiful websites. Diversifying boosted revenue 25 percent, and suddenly we were attracting the best designers. Our presentation work remained strong, but not our focus.

Then, BAM! The dot-com bubble burst, followed by 9/11. That extra revenue disappeared almost overnight. We lost another 25 percent due to reduced client spending.

During those tough times, Jim Collins published what is my favorite business book of all time: *Good to Great*. He said that if there's one thing you are passionate about, can be best in the world at, and make money at, do that one thing. *Ding!*

We flipped our strategy, declared that we would become the best in the world in the niche area of presentation design, and never looked back. We cut web and print out completely. We turned all other work away. Crazy to do that in tough times, right?

But our goal was to move presentation from a reviled medium to one that people believe can change the world. We channeled all our creative energy into changing the perception of presentations. Every transformative movement begins with the spoken word—that presentations got no respect from the perspective of design just didn't seem right.

If we had not said no to the other work, today we'd be indistinguishable from all the other agencies out there. Instead, I couldn't be more proud of the fact that we've achieved what we set out to do: change how the world communicates through presentations.

That's the power of no.

Nancy Duarte (duarte.com) is the cofounder of Duarte Design and the author most recently of Resonate. *She has designed over 250,000 presentations.*

CONFIDENCE TO SUBTRACT

Scott Belsky

Subtraction shows up in our product development process. We've developed these tools for creatives to showcase their work online. You'd think those products over time would have more features, more options, more functionality. When I look back, in fact we kept removing things.

With maturity has come this mantra with the development team of reduction and simplification. And now we have data on how people are actually using our products, and it's amazing. When you reduce the number of doors that someone can walk through, more people walk through the one that you want them to walk through.

It seems obvious, but as anyone who creates products for a living knows, it's natural and instinctive to want to give people more choices and options so that you can attract a larger audience. In other words, you build a door for each type of person—the opposite of reducing the number of doors.

As user experience becomes more important and people try to go beyond the product or service to create an experience, I think there's a real argument for reducing the number of options, choices, and features.

It's made a huge difference for us at Behance.

Part of what drove it was confidence in the service we are providing. In the early days, we didn't really know exactly how people would benefit from what we were doing. When you aren't sure about what you're really good at, you start to layer on all sorts of different elements because you are hedging yourself.

In our case, for example, we had this thing called Creative Forum where people could have open conversations; we added a thing called Tip Exchange where creative people could exchange career tips; we added Groups so that people could congregate by interest; and we had a portfolio showcase so you could follow people's work. And *that*, we realized, was the essence of Behance: allowing people to showcase and discover creative work.

Everything else was a distraction from that core offering.

When you're confident, you begin to subtract. You begin to focus on the key things you're most proud of rather than having that safe and scattered strategy where you're adding more and more stuff just to hedge your product, your service, yourself.

And as you subtract, you become more confident.

Scott Belsky is the founder and CEO of Behance and the bestselling author of Making Ideas Happen*.*
(Photo: Julia Soler)

APPRECIATION OVER ACCUMULATION

Stephen Shapiro

Over a decade ago, I moved from a four-bedroom house in the New Jersey suburbs to a furnished one-bedroom apartment in the heart of London. With a considerably smaller residential space and an international move to contend with, downsizing was inevitable. Surprisingly, I got rid of nearly everything I owned and was able to fit all of my possessions in just two boxes. It was during this transition that I learned the freedom associated with owning less. Heck, when it was time to move apartments while in London, I was able to do so in the back of a taxi with only two trips.

This minimalistic approach has numerous side benefits.

Owning less means fewer things that can break, get lost, or need dusting.

On a more personal level, I tend to be disorganized, so having less "stuff" means less clutter. And less clutter in my physical world creates less clutter in my head. This "space" allows me to be more creative, which in turn has led to greater professional success.

Keeping my possessions to a minimum also allows me to keep my financial obligations to a minimum. I still live in a relatively inexpensive one-bedroom apartment, now in Boston. Although necessity may be the mother of invention, not worrying about paying the bills is the father of entrepreneurship. My simple lifestyle means that I can earn less while still maintaining financial security. This simplicity also lends itself to flexibility and freedom. If I need to relocate again, I won't feel locked in or constrained.

When I buy new clothes (which is not often), I donate something from my closet to charity. In fact, I keep all of my purchases to a minimum because I have experienced the value of my metaphorical two boxes.

We are a society built on "having what we want." We are always striving for more. But there is power in "wanting what we have." Start with a deep sense of gratitude for your life as it is now. Recognize that happiness does not lie in the achievement of some future goal that may or may not ever come to fruition.

Happiness begins today. When you stop accumulating and start appreciating, you create more freedom, flexibility, creativity, and inner peace.

Stephen Shapiro (steveshapiro.com) is an innovation consultant and the author most recently of Best Practices Are Stupid: 40 Ways to Out-Innovate the Competition.

INTO THE LIGHT

Jon Miller

 When I first began helping companies do *kaizen*—"good change"— it was all about opening up the bursting basket of improvement tools and designing more rational processes. It was a thrilling intellectual challenge to grasp the situation, grapple with human resistance to change, and guide the organization to better things. Nearly two decades later, I'm a little wiser, and my approach to *kaizen* is more about less.

I used to think ignorance was a space to be filled with knowledge, skills, and elegant systems. Now I see it as something akin to dark matter: often invisible and only accounted for by the effect it has on everything around it. Ignorance is no longer an absence of knowledge; it is a definite presence that must be removed. But there is more than one type of ignorance.

One type of ignorance is the misconception, often disguised as a well-formed opinion, theory, or understanding. Applied to the real world, these may even *appear* to hold true. We may continue to apply our misconceived model for years or decades, surviving on luck or a forgiving environment. However, when faced with the test of the scientific method, misconceptions are forced to yield to empirical fact.

The scientific method is not the imposition of one idea in place of another. It is the attempt to disprove a null hypothesis, to subtract that option as being truth. Misconceptions or incorrect knowledge fail to survive well-designed scientific experiments. *Kaizen*, science, and innovation are all subtraction of many failed experiments, not the pursuit of the successful one.

Another type of ignorance, though, is more insidious, pervasive, and difficult to remove. Called variously confirmation bias, prejudice, or willful ignorance, it is a force that acts on the rational mind to deny reality in place of a reality that is somehow more personally favorable. There are no winning arguments or ways to remove willful ignorance by force of logic, rarely any addition of information that can displace it.

The root cause for the existence of the willful ignorance must be identified and removed. It is typically an emotion such as fear, greed, anger, or even love. These are hardly the domain of the traditional businessperson or engineer, but they are the frontier.

This is a long way to come from happily applying basketfuls of industrial engineering tools to pliant processes. People can be taught many things in school, at work, and in life.

If we can teach them to actively identify and remove ignorance, we will have achieved a great thing.

Jon Miller (gembapantarei.com) is the CEO of Kaizen Institute, a global consultancy dedicated to helping good companies become world-class organizations. He was born and raised in Japan.

LAW <u>NO.</u> 2

THE SIMPLEST RULES

CREATE THE MOST

EFFECTIVE EXPERIENCE

Let it be.
John Lennon and Paul McCartney

True story.

I'm standing on top of the Arc de Triomphe in Paris, looking down at the chaotic traffic circle that surrounds it, scared out of my wits. I know that in three days' time I will have no choice but to navigate my way around what can only be described as an endless loop of sheer madness. My wife and daughter are with me for a two-week European trip combining business and pleasure, and we have decided to rent a car and drive out to the chateaus in the French countryside for a few days of quiet time. We are staying at a hotel just a half block away from the arc, off the Champs Élysées, and the only way out is through the traffic circle. Were I not about to join the insanity a few days hence, the ludicrous following scene would be hilarious.

Twelve well-trafficked avenues that feed into the unmarked, uncontrolled circle make for a relentless onslaught of high-volume traffic moving at what appears to be dangerously high speeds. There are no lines, lanes, or lights on the Place de l'Étoile, which is the street name of the circle. The flow is constant. Although tiny bands of teenage boys dart back and forth across the cobbles in a death-defying game of dodge car that's clearly no concern of the police officers stationed at many of the entry points, the only way for pedestrians to get safely to the Arc de Triomphe is through a tunnel running underneath the street. Never once over the last several days have I seen a letup in either volume or speed. I've driven through roundabouts and rotaries in other European countries and dozens in the New England states, as well as New York City's Columbus Circle, but none like this one, none in a modern metropolis with that many cars and that many major streets feeding in.

My first thought: This is crazy. How can it possibly work?

The travel journalist Rick Steves wrote in a 2009 column for the online version of *Smithsonian* magazine, "In the mid-19th century, Baron Haussmann set out to make Paris the grandest city in Europe. The twelve arterials that radiate from the Arc de Triomphe were part of his master plan: the creation of a series of major boulevards, intersecting at diagonals with monuments as centerpieces [such as the Arc de Triomphe] . . . it's obvious that Haussmann's plan did not anticipate the automobile."

Yet it works. It works very well. The more I watch, the more it seems familiar. I remember television personality John Stossel's "Spontaneous Order" video of him and the Olympian Brian Boitano, obviously a subject matter expert, standing in the middle with a megaphone, trying to lead, control, and direct the skaters in a rink—only to cause a few to fall. It dawns on me that the cars circling the arc are exhibiting the same spontaneous order with amazing effectiveness. Having that familiar metaphor in mind helps quell my fear. I take heart and decide to become a student of the driving patterns so that when it comes time to test my hand behind the wheel and face the circle, it won't seem so daunting.

I plant myself across from the arc for a few hours while my wife and daughter stroll the Champs Élysées, "window shopping." (This, it turns out, is not a subtractive activity by any stretch of the imagination.) I'm determined to observe and decipher the rules of the road. In an exercise in futility, I try asking people what the rules are. Most shake their heads at me, which I take to mean either "crazy American" or "no rules," depending on their body language. To my eye, the circle doesn't work right at all.

Other than the fact that traffic flows counterclockwise as is the norm, it's all wrong.

In every other roundabout I've ever been through, right-of-way is given to those already in the circle. In the Arc de Triomphe traffic circle, those entering the circle have right-of-way. That rule is simple enough, but it doesn't make immediate sense and isn't posted anywhere. On the basis of that simple rule, it seems that once you're in the circular flow, you basically don't exist to other drivers and have to act accordingly. That also means that if you're on the left, you don't exist, and if you want to survive, you better keep a wary eye out for those on the right. It's utterly and completely the opposite of every other traffic circle on the planet.

My observations prove to be correct.

The day comes when I have to pick up my rental car, which I do, but not without asking about insurance coverage for accidents in the circle around the arc. Interestingly, the French take a no fault view of things when it comes to incidents in the circle: it's an automatic assumption that both parties are to blame, and claims are split in half. Emboldened, I immediately take a test drive around the city, saving my test run around the arc for last. Traveling around the arc for the first time with wife and daughter on board is simply not an option; I need at least a little confidence. I wait at the light on the Champs Élysées—nearly all twelve entry avenues have lights— then take off without hesitation on green.

I get honked at immediately but ignore it. I move into the middle of the flow and become supervigilant, not unlike the way one would navigate around a crowded ice rink. Self-interest and self-preservation allow the order to emerge. I circumnavigate the circle a half dozen times and begin to feel comfortable. It's actually starting to be fun: I feel completely present and focused and aware of everything around me, the exact opposite of my style and frame of mind while driving on the streets of suburban Los Angeles, where I live and where my thinking is admittedly dulled and my attention diluted. It comes time to exit, which I know will be the biggest challenge, because I have no right-of-way whatsoever. Knowing that keeps me on edge and calls on every reflex I have. I exit without incident but not without a few "oh, crap!" moments.

I make it safely and securely to the hotel, gather the family, take a spin around the arc like a pro, and head out to the country. We travel through dozens of roundabouts, all laden with heavy signage, all working in the reverse of the Arc de Triomphe, all a mere fraction of its size and flow. We happen upon one fairly serious accident involving three cars and have two near misses ourselves. In fact, over the course of a full seven days in France, the only incidents, accidents, and gridlock I see or experience happen in the presence of a multitude of traditional traffic controls intended to prevent those very situations.

I marvel at how never once was there anything but constant, incident-free flow around the Arc de Triomphe.

My experience introduces and bears testament to the second law of subtraction: *The simplest rules create the most effective experience.*

The effect of any experience is determined by how actively engaged we are as we move through time and space in a particular setting. The way we perceive these two dimensions—how they land on us in a specific event and how we interpret the feeling we get—is what gives the elements of time and space real meaning. The more enjoyable, expedient, and efficient an experience is, the more meaning we give it.

Movement through time and space in a particular setting is the subject of this chapter. When you focus on these elements of experience, you begin to think differently. You begin to search for natural and self-organizing patterns of human behavior. You begin to wonder how to exploit those patterns for good rather than just control them. You discover that the most effective experience can be achieved not by demanding that people comply with a mandate from on high or conform to an exhaustive set of rigid regulations but by following one or two simple rules. You realize that those simple rules can often emerge from the right context, need not be stated to be understood by everyone, and produce the highest levels of participation. You understand that telling people what to do isn't nearly as effective as inspiring them what to do. This is the stuff of meaning.

Such is the case with things such as traffic on roads and streets, how much we get done in groups and meetings, and the environments in which we perform our work. We spend most of our waking hours in those three settings.

How effective are those experiences?

END OF THE ROAD

My Paris driving experience raises a number of questions. The Arc de Triomphe was planned without considering automobiles, whereas more modern, technologically advanced, yet much less effective urban planning always must take them into account. How is it that a seemingly chaotic construct can work so well? How can you act on that insight to reproduce an engaging and effective experience, but in a different setting and perhaps in way that doesn't feel quite so risky and dangerous?

A "shared space" transformation occurring under the auspices of the Royal Borough of Kensington and Chelsea in London helps answer these questions. Shared space is an urban design concept that rests on a simple premise: roads and streets are different beasts. A road is for automobiles only, but a street is for everyone; a street is a place of integration, not of segregation. Roads are meant to allow vehicles to bypass the congested city via high-speed routing. Streets are to be shared equally by all who travel within a city space, without giving priority or assigning right-of-way to any single kind of traveler.

It's a different way of thinking.

Shared space is easily recognized. It's a street space where all traditional traffic controls—lights, lanes, lines, signs, and barriers—have been removed. Curbing is removed to blur the lines between pedestrian and vehicular travel. The philosophy is that the absence of all those features produces a more user-friendly social context, one that gives rise to a self-organizing equilibrium governed only by human interaction.

It's the artful, thoughtful, humane version of what happens on Place de l'Étoile around the Arc de Triomphe.

And it works incredibly well.

Shared space rests on the idea that traditional traffic controls partition distinct spaces and allocate them to the different modes of travel but create a false sense of security for each user. That causes people to stop thinking and to behave as if they had no responsibility to look out for other users in "their" space. Shared space removes those designations, rights, and priorities, replacing them with a setting that creates shared responsibility and allows a more effective and equitable experience to emerge.

I was aware of shared space as an experimental design idea, the brain-child of the late traffic engineer Hans Monderman, in Dutch towns and villages. Monderman's work over three decades was successful in Holland, often doubling traffic flow and halving the number of accidents. Shared space is no longer an experiment. It's a movement that is well under way. Over 400 European locations have adopted it, but it is in the United Kingdom that the most significant progress is being made.

A SENSE OF PLACE

It's one thing to redesign a village intersection that gets under 10,000 daily traffic crossings; it's quite another to reimagine a large metropolitan space that sees more visitors annually than the entire city of Venice, Italy.

Introducing Exhibition Road, an ambitious £29 million shared space project that commenced on February 11, 2009, with an act of subtraction: royal commissioners removed a curbstone as a symbol of the future single-surface street. Work was completed December 8, 2011, on time and on budget.

I witnessed the construction in November 2010 and learned the particulars from urban designers Hamilton-Baillie Associates, project architects Dixon Jones Architects, and the Royal Borough of Kensington and Chelsea.

The goal was to return Exhibition Road to its beginnings and use shared space urban design to turn it into an engaging streetscape that would be a focal point for visitors to the 2012 Olympic and Paralympic Games. It was literally the end of the road as Londoners knew it.

The story is a study in subtraction.

Exhibition Road runs from the South Kensington tube station on the south up to Cromwell Road bordering Hyde Park on the north. The road is home to a unique collection of important British cultural and educational institutions, including the Victoria and Albert Museum, the Natural History Museum, the Science Museum, Holy Trinity Church, the Royal Albert Hall, the Royal Geographical Society, the Royal College of Art, the English National Ballet, Hyde Park Chapel, and Imperial College London. Since the Great Exhibition of 1851, Exhibition Road has been a major destination and attracts over 11 million visitors each year, added to the 7 million regular users: students, local workers, and residents.

Here's what it looked like in 2008, before work began.

The mission, according to the Royal Borough of Kensington and Chelsea, was to transform Exhibition Road into "the most accessible cultural destination in the world."

No easy feat, that. There wasn't much more you could add to the space. It had every kind of modern traffic control firmly in place. People weren't happy, though, and neither was the borough, calling it an "unwelcoming road" that was "filled with street clutter and vehicle traffic" and "confusing to visitors and unfriendly to pedestrians."

The old way wasn't working. Exhibition Road needed something more than a cosmetic treatment. It needed a complete overhaul to become a completely new space—an inviting, vital, and living streetscape—with a sense of place. It needed a new vision.

Enter shared space design.

The firm of Hamilton-Baillie Associates was brought in to help reenvision Exhibition Road. The principal, Ben Hamilton-Baillie, drew on his experience working with Hans Monderman in the Dutch experiments and his familiarity with dozens of successful smaller shared space projects in the United Kingdom.

Around the market town of Ashford in Kent, for example, the firm transformed a former three-lane, high-speed one-way inner ring road into a low-speed shared space where pedestrians now interact informally with the 12,000 vehicles that continue to use the streets each day. Before Exhibition Road, the Ashford scheme was the largest and most ambitious one in Europe, turning one kilometer of the former ring road into a very different model for town center streets. Traffic signals, guardrails, and all road markings were removed, replaced by a series of distinctive places at each intersection and linked by simple boulevards of visually narrowed carriageways that are bisected by informal "courtesy crossings."

Hamilton-Baillie erased all distinction between road and pavement, resurfacing the street with cobblestones to provide a textured surface that results in reduced vehicle speeds and encourages more informal pedestrian crossings. The firm had a local artist redesign shallow drainage gullies with new lighting and street furniture. The first 15 months of operation saw average traffic speeds drop close to 20 miles per hour, accompanied a drop in accidents and injuries to zero, with but one scraped knee on record. In mid-July 2009, the *London Evening Standard* called Ashford in Kent "the most progressive [town] in England. The roads have acquired a new dignity and people comment on a new sense of community and courtesy."

Where the Streets Have No End

As work began on Exhibition Road, the British press took up the torch. Simon Jenkins of the *London Evening Standard* made an eloquent case for shared space in mid-July 2009, defending it in an online argument against a few local residents whose feathers were ruffled by the construction and who had organized a minor protest.

"We are conditioned to assume that, because cars are big and fast, they cannot co-exist with other road users," wrote Jenkins, and went on to say that those cars are "driven by people with eyes and ears. They become lethal only when drivers are turned into zombies by concentrating on signs above and below their normal line of vision. They race as fast as they can between lights and crossings."

It was as if Jenkins were channeling both Hans Monderman and Ben Hamilton-Baillie, as I'd heard both gentlemen make the same argument before, using nearly identical words.

Jenkins went on to argue that shared or "naked" streets, as he termed them, regard vehicles as "people on wheels." According to Jenkins, "They have a right to a share of public space, though not in any unique or privileged sense. For half a century vehicles have been treated as metallic things, to be disciplined and dragooned by traffic engineers, with a forest of signs, lights, one-way streets, kerbs, railings, crossings, and general delay. As a result, drivers have no time or incentive to negotiate space with other street users. They just bully their way across town as directed by the engineers."

He went on to say correctly that most accident spots are near bus and cycle lanes, school gates, and zebra crossings; in other words, places where traffic is supposedly the most highly regulated and thus controlled and supposedly safe.

"The regulation merely leads to drivers being distracted," wrote Jenkins. "By making everyone feel safer, the engineers have made them less so. It is a classic of health-and-safety dirigisme, stripping all street users of personal reliance and responsibility and causing accidents as a result. The most dangerous people in London are the road engineers. They encourage drivers to kill people."

Those are not gentle words. Jenkins is obviously not one for pulling punches.

Jenkins made a succinct and accurate closing argument by writing that shared space removes all street clutter and visual distraction. "The street is deliberately made to seem more confused, 'policed' informally by the eyes and ears of its users. Cyclists and jaywalkers go from being the most anarchic and accident-prone road users to being the most effective policemen. The Kensington and Chelsea council may have the most archaic residents parking in London but on traffic management it is a knight in shining armor."

Observe First, Design Second

The most interesting aspect of Exhibition Road isn't what was eventually done but the process behind the way the design elements were conceived.

It comes as no surprise that Hamilton-Baillie Associates began with a solid *genchi genbutsu*. As Ben Hamilton-Baillie told me, "What's wrong with how we engineer things is that most of what we accept as the proper order of things is based on assumptions, not observations. If we observed first, designed second, we wouldn't need most of the things we build."

As with any good designer, Ben's creative process is hard to pin down, and it should be, since creative thinking is anything but a linear, step-by-step method. But as an annoying writer is obligated to do, I asked the question anyway.

"I can't really describe or pin down our creative process in approaching a project," Ben begins. "Each one is so different! The key thing about our approach is to understand the sense of place and the particular characteristics of a town, a village, a street, or even an intersection. We tend to focus on things that most traffic engineers ignore: history, morphology, landscape, climate, geology, economic history, as well as making sure that we observe and listen carefully to any clues or observations offered. Allowing people to talk is important; even if what they say is not necessarily relevant to the issues in hand, talking is good."

What exactly is sense of place, and why does it matter? As Ben explains it, "Places evolve and are shaped by movement. Travel to and from and around places, and the reasons for those journeys, shapes our past and our future usage. Movement patterns mold and define places and help explain their form. Those patterns change over time. Understanding such changes and their effects helps explain the increasing dominance of movement in many villages and offers clues to reestablishing the principles of place."

In other words, the past helps explain the present and lights the future. Every place—town, village, road, and intersection—is unique. Building a clear picture of the current space and situation has everything to do with being clear about what the future may offer. "You have to consider the broad picture as well as the detail," Ben says. "Why is the place the way it is? How did it develop in the past? How do people respond to it today? Understanding the history and context, along with the distinctive features and characteristics of a place, provides us with a foundation for a successful plan, which is always built on a deep understanding of the special qualities and circumstances that combine to create an individual place."

Ben looks at everything, starting with historical maps, materials in local history societies, and historical records, to help explain the origins and development of a place. He looks at how the character of the surrounding landscape is shaped by the soils, the geology, and the land use activities that originally supported the inhabitants of the settlement. He studies how social and economic forces and events may have influenced the patterns of land use and the location of buildings and spaces. "Most places will have been shaped by combinations of these and many other factors," he says. "Sketching out the evolution of a town or village can help explain and illustrate its character and form. An understanding of the history helps when it comes to finding ways to emphasize character and context in the eventual redesign."

Wanting the nitty-gritty details, I dig a bit more into that sketch. An actual detailed hand-drawn sketch of the current place is always developed to provide a visual reference and explain the current character. The goal is to produce a mental as well as physical map that becomes a useful companion in helping to define the way a place is perceived and understood. "If possible, encourage children to draw a plan of the place, especially in a town or village, based on their day-to-day experience," Ben advises. "They seem to be able to catch the small details that often go unremarked or unnoticed."

Part of the Hamilton-Baillie tool kit is a 10-point audit to make sure those vital details aren't overlooked. The list consists of road signs and signals; directional signs and signposts; road markings such as center lines, stop lines, and parking restraints; pavements and curb details; railings, guardrails, and bollards; paving materials and surfacing and where they change; street lighting and other light sources; advertising signs and hoardings; bus stops and taxi ranks; and service covers, gullies, and drains.

Understanding the moving parts is obviously critical. A virtual peek over the urban designer's shoulder reveals that there's no secret to observing and recording the patterns of pedestrian movement: you sit and watch a place during the busiest hours and mark each person's route with a thin line on the sketch. You note where people walk and where they cross the street. You circle the places where people stop or pause, where they linger or rest, and where they interact with others. You do that for a few hours and then look at your sketch: the clustering of lines and circles illuminates the patterns of movement and lines of human travel.

You move on to vehicular movement, manually counting numbers of passing vehicles per hour. You track trucks, cars, motorcycles, and bicycles. You perform counts during a typical morning rush hour, one during the middle of a weekday, and one on a Saturday. You multiply the vehicle flow during a peak hour by 10 to get a daily estimate of vehicles per day.

Recording speeds is a bit trickier; the easiest and simplest way is to drive through the place in light traffic and record typical speeds from your speedometer readings to create a fairly accurate picture. You do that at different times of day and pay close attention to approaches, entries, and exits. You mark up the sketch with different colors to denote the speed profile of the place, calling out or highlighting areas where speeds tend to be higher or lower.

The collective input makes for a thorough shared space *genchi genbutsu*. Next come the ideas about what to remove. "We use Photoshop or something similar to remove extraneous elements from our initial photographs and sketches in order to strip back to what is important," Ben tells me. "We subtract the road markings, road signs, overhead power lines, advertisements, and any clutter. It allows us to see the basic structure and skeletal form of a place more clearly and usually throws up possibilities for emphasizing the sense of place."

When it comes to movement through space and time—the experience—the ideal speed profile is a primary consideration and gets careful thought. "The question is, What speeds feel reasonably comfortable and safe?" poses Ben. "You have to resist the temptation to assume that the slowest speed is the target. Slowest doesn't necessarily equate to optimal speed." Ben recommends speeds in the range of 15 to 20 mph for two reasons: safety and flow.

Safety First

Safety analysts such as the National Highway Transportation Safety Association in the United States have known for decades that the maximum vehicle speed at which pedestrians can escape severe injury upon impact is just under 20 miles per hour.

What's magic about 20 mph? A few things. First, there's the hypothesis by E. O. Wilson that the "maximum theoretical running speed" for humans is 20 mph. "This suggests that our physiology and psychology has evolved based around the potential maximum impact on the speed of human beings," states Ben.

That may also explain why flow is better at less than 20 mph. "It's in this range that drivers can respond easily to their surroundings," Ben explains. "Above 25 mph pedestrians and cyclists are much less comfortable, and informal communication through gestures and eye contact becomes harder. Humans can read a huge amount in each other with only a fraction of a second of eye contact. That's one reason shared spaces work so well—people tell each other what maneuvers they're planning with just a glance."

The interplay between speed, traffic controls, and overall flow is interesting. "The optimal speed is the one that allows all vehicles to flow smoothly and steadily through the space without excessive braking or acceleration," Ben says. "All the data show that when speeds slow to around 20 mph, traffic flow improves and congestion disappears."

This puzzles many people, although mathematically it's not surprising, according to Ben: "Your speed of journey, the ability of traffic to move smoothly through the built environment, depends on the performance of your intersections, not on your speed of flow between intersections. Intersections work more efficiently at lower speeds. At 30 miles per hour, you need control systems like traffic signals, which themselves mean that the intersection is not in use for significant periods of time. But at slower speeds, vehicles can be much closer together and drivers can use eye contact to engage and make decisions. So you get much higher capacity."

The exhaustive homework culminates in prototype sketches like these that depict the primary features of what redesigned space might look like:

Market Cross, or other feature, with seating contribute to reducing vehicle speed.

Market Stalls in the street

Paving & kerbs appropriate to the context & pedestrian usage

informal parking

tree planting where practical

Change in road surface

Bollards (used sparingly) reinforce speed reduction

End of road markings

APPROACHING THE CENTRE OF THE VILLAGE / TOWN

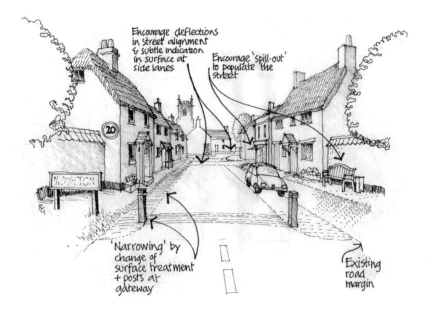

Encourage deflections in street alignment & subtle indication in surface at side lanes

Encourage 'spill-out' to populate the street

'Narrowing' by change of surface treatment + posts at gateway

Existing road margin

The plans for Exhibition Road followed a similar approach, incorporating all the features of a typical shared space design. Courtesy of Dixon Jones Architects and the Royal Borough of Kensington and Chelsea, here are a couple of the early designer sketches:

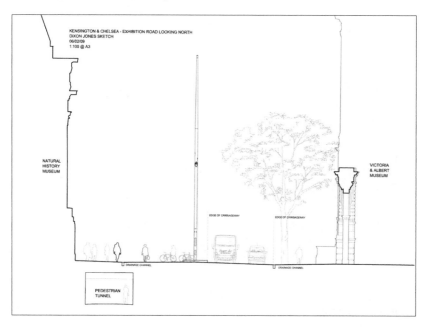

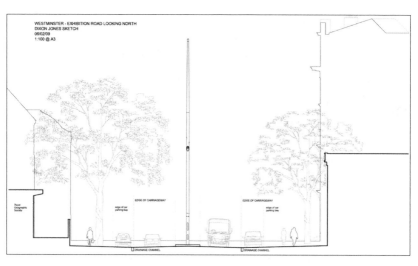

And courtesy of photographer Paul Riddle (paul-riddle.com) for Dixon Jones Architects, here is the new Exhibition Road:

The Royal Borough of Kensington and Chelsea describes the new Exhibition Road this way on its website:

> A distinctive chequered granite street design that features a single surface runs from South Kensington Station to Hyde Park and the full width of the road from building to building. The busiest section of Exhibition Road for pedestrians is between South Kensington and Prince Consort Road. This is where most visitors walk to the museums. In this part of the road there is a four metre wide corridor from the buildings on the western side which is a safe area for pedestrians. Next to this there is an eight metre transition zone where there are parking bays, cycle racks and other items of street furniture. This is followed by two lanes for traffic, one each way, then a four metre pedestrian zone on the eastern side of the road.
>
> We have removed kerbs, barriers and street clutter so pedestrians can move around the area more freely, particularly those using wheelchairs, motorised buggies and pushchairs. Black cast iron drainage

channel covers run along each side of Exhibition Road, about four metres out from the respective building lines. Alongside the drainage channels, strips of corduroy tactile warn blind and partially sighted people that they are moving into or out of vehicle free areas. Tall, sleek street lighting masts have been specifically designed to complement the grand buildings of Exhibition Road and provide a safe and welcoming nocturnal environment for residents and visitors.

Show Time

As work on Exhibition Road neared completion in November 2011, Justin McGuirk of *The Guardian*, in a piece called "A Farewell to Pavements," applauded the project, focusing on the key principle of shared space—simple rules: "Rules are one of the hallmarks of civilization, and in a civilized society, most people abide by them. Rules, after all, are our invisible prophylactic against chaos. Except that rules are not always invisible—they also take physical form. Roads and pavements are rules, keeping hard cars and soft pedestrians apart. Lane markings, pedestrian crossings and steel railings are another layer of rules. Do we really need such nannying? What if we relaxed the rules a little?"

Relaxed they were. The transformation of Exhibition Road was deemed so successful that it was chosen as the site of a spectacular festival called Road Show during the first week of the 2012 Olympic Games and became a destination for visitors. The event featured the work of emerging young performers and allowed both Londoners and visitors to relax and recharge during the Olympics. The new streetscape included games, dance, scientific experiments and debates, music, acrobatics and aerial displays, new writers' commissions, and visual art installations. Special customized trailers housed many festival elements to preserve both the new streetscape and access for residents.

The Exhibition Road experience is not only a good example of how the simplest rules create the most effective experience but also an explicit example of how to subtract the obvious and add the meaningful.

SPOTLIGHT ON

SPOTLIGHT ON
SIMPLE RULES

People love to make collages. We learn to do it as children. It's fun, simple, and easy: you collect photographs, cut them with scissors, arrange them in creative ways, and paste them down. It's a wonderful way to create great art out of photos and other images. It gets really enjoyable when you sit around a table with a pile of random photos and make collages with friends.

Perhaps that's why people love Mixel, the iPad app created by former NYTimes.com design director Khoi Vinh. Mixel is the world's first social collage app: it lets you make, share, and remix collages, called mixels, with your friends. The tools are intentionally spare and imprecise yet so simple and the experience is so intuitive and creative that users describe it as "addicting."

You start with an image, which can come from anywhere: your photo library, the web, Facebook. You use your finger to draw a crop line around the part of the image you want to play with and move the images around to create your collage. When you're done, you post it for your friends. When they see what you've created, they can "like," comment on, and share your mixel. The magic happens when they open it up, see how you did it, and remix it, reworking your original pieces into a new creative collage.

Mixel lets you remix anything you see—you may see parts of your mixels show up in those of others—and organizes those remixes into threads. The threads become highly engaging visual conversations that anyone can join. The power of the Mixel experience revolves not around technique, not around art, but around *art as conversation*.

What's missing from Mixel? The price. It's free.

LET IT BE

You don't need to understand chaos and complexity theory to see why shared space works. You don't need the "beautiful mind" of the theoretical mathematician John Nash to see why equilibrium is achieved efficiently in a shared space. You don't need to have a game theorist's understanding of the prisoner's dilemma to understand why effective cooperation occurs in a shared space. You just need to understand that the universe is characterized by a natural order that is emergent, self-organizing, and adaptive.

Chaos theory tells us that everything in the natural world—from microorganisms to weather patterns to the growth of populations—is a part of a complex system that is moving toward equilibrium. Just because something looks chaotic or unorganized, that doesn't mean it is. The traffic patterns around the Arc de Triomphe emerge from the convergence of mostly random forces to form what is in reality a higher-order behavior than that of the overregulated roads feeding into it.

But the impatient human mind seeks order and symmetry, and when we don't see it immediately, we are compelled to quickly impose it. It's when in our impatience we fail to look beyond the obvious that we rush in with our rigid regulations and hierarchies in an attempt to control what is already in balance; in the process, we tip things the other way and get the exact opposite of what we really want.

When we do that, we exhibit a level of intelligence below that of a slime mold. In his 2001 book *Emergence: The Connected Lives of Ants, Brains, Cities, and Software*, Steven B. Johnson discussed the 1960s studies of slime mold by Mitch Resnick. It turns out that the slime is not one big smear of an organism oozing toward food on the floor; it's really a multitude of single-cell microorganisms working together toward a greater purpose. In other words, slime mold displays a collective intelligence that people often don't.

But if you know where to look and what to look for, you can find great examples of just the opposite: when we let things be, provide the right context, and allow nature to produce a self-organizing experience as effective as that of shared space.

The Unpolicy

As Daniel Pink pointed out in a 2010 column for *The Telegraph,* the vacation policy employed by Netflix, the streaming video and DVD-by-mail company based in Silicon Valley, "is audaciously simple and simply audacious. Salaried employees can take as much time off as they'd like, whenever they want to take it. Nobody—not employees themselves, not managers—tracks vacation days. In other words, Netflix's holiday policy is to have no policy at all."

It hasn't always been that way. In 2004, Netflix treated holidays the conventional way: everyone got a set number of days each year, used them, or worked the system to get paid for time not taken.

"But eventually some employees recognized that this arrangement was at odds with how they really did their jobs," says Pink. "After all, they were responding to e-mails on weekends, they were solving problems online at home at night. Since Netflix wasn't tracking how many hours people were logging each work day, these employees wondered, why should it track how many holidays people were taking each work year? Fair point, said management. So the company scrapped its formal plan."

"Rules and policies and regulations and stipulations are innovation killers. People do their best work when they're unencumbered," says Pink, quoting Steve Swasey, Netflix's vice president of corporate communication. "If you're spending a lot of time accounting for the time you're spending, that's time you're not innovating."

The Unmeeting

Following rigidly set agenda schedules in highly structured meetings, strategic off-site retreats, and action-planning sessions is the norm for most business organizations. Conferences and company summits are generally chock full of tightly scripted gatherings with attendance mandated, issues outlined, and people assigned. More often than not, little in the way of collective thought and action toward a common purpose gets done. Attendees generally agree that the best part of these events takes place in the free time set aside for informal gathering. That's when people connect with one another, forge new connections, and share the ideas they're most passionate about.

One of the most effective means of conducting meetings exploits that social aspect and points it toward complex challenges, using an approach called Open Space Technology (OST). The label is a misnomer, as technology plays no part in the process. In fact, at an OST meeting there are no formal presentations, no formal agendas, no keynote speakers, no panel discussions, and no trade show elements of any kind. Instead, the conference content emerges from the participants in attendance at the opening circle, guided only by the requirement that if you attend, you must be passionate about the overall theme and willing to take responsibility for action items created with that energy. Issues of concern related to the general theme get raised and posted on the wall at the outset, and participants then head off to the spaces and places reserved for them.

With OST, the self-organizing principles at play are these: (1) whoever comes are the right people, (2) whatever happens is the only thing that could have, (3) whenever it starts is the right time, and (4) when it is over, it is over.

There is one simple rule, called the Law of Two Feet, which is essentially that you let your feet do the voting: if you find yourself in a situation where you aren't learning or contributing, you go somewhere else. The rule creates an experience that appears chaotic yet is anything but. No one is in control; rather, everyone is. Having used the method successfully a number of times—it requires no expertise of any kind—I can attest to how enjoyable, creative, and productive an OST event is.

Harrison Owen coined the term *Open Space* in 1984, when he discovered the effectiveness of using an agendaless, leaderless format to engage a heterogeneous group of people around a complex issue. As he puts it:

> You're wondering how Open Space happened? Well, it's very simple. I needed to convene a large conference, and I didn't have any time. I was having a drink, wondering how I was going to do this. By the time I finished my second drink, it was pretty clear that what we ought to do is sit in a circle, because that's the way people get together, in a

circle. And then we'd create a bulletin board so they could say what it was they wanted to talk about. And we'd open a marketplace so they could figure out where and when they wanted to meet. And then we'd go to work. And that's when my cocktail was over. And that's Open Space: sit in a circle, create a bulletin board, open a marketplace, and go to work. It's probably been done two or three hundred thousand times in 124 countries around the world, and I suspect it's been used in just about any situation you can imagine. I've used it with Boeing Aircraft redesigning manufacturing processes. It's used in the Middle East to bring conflicted parties together; I've done some of that. Goat herders in India creating an agricultural co-op; there are thousands and thousands of applications.

The Unoffice

The term *shared space* is . . . shared. It's the term Toronto's Centre for Social Innovation (CSI) now uses for the community workspaces it creates. The internationally recognized center defines a social innovation as "an idea that works for the public good" and focuses on creating new spaces to catalyze and support social innovation.

CSI's publication *Shared Spaces for Social Innovation* states: "There is increasing recognition that the problems we face are too complex to be addressed by any single player. Shared spaces connect diverse organizations and individuals, giving them the chance to collaborate, share knowledge and develop systemic solutions to the issues they are trying to address. Shared workspaces are themselves a social innovation—an entirely new way of working. The dominant workplace model has been separate organizations working separately. That may have made perfect sense at one time and it may still make perfect sense in many instances. But it is by no means a universal or desirable approach. The nature of work is changing—and with it the workplace."

In other words, CSI creates the conditions and context for social innovation to emerge, using space designed with intentions similar to those of the urban design version as well as those of OST: allow people to feel comfortable in a space, help them develop relationships with others doing the same thing, and enable mutually beneficial interactions to emerge.

The theory is that a workspace thoughtfully designed with collaboration in mind produces a community, and "community is what leads to innovation, because a community of other creative, engaged people is what blows away the cobwebs, allows you to see an old problem in a new light, and helps you find creative ways of implementing solutions you might not otherwise have considered."

The Unleader

If you search YouTube and watch "Who Needs Leaders?" you can see Nick Obolensky, author of *Complex Adaptive Leadership*, quickly put complexity to work and demonstrate the power of emergent self-organization. Nick takes a couple dozen people who are scattered around a large room and asks them to organize themselves according to a single simple rule: silently pick any two other people in the group and position yourself an equal distance from both.

The group moves about the room in seemingly chaotic fashion at first, yet a pattern quickly emerges and an equilibrium is established in just under a minute. Nick congratulates them and then asks, "What would have happened if we had put one of you in charge?" The room erupts with laughter, and the video ends.

By now you know why they laughed. Still, since it was a great exercise and demonstrated the point of Law 2 so well, I contacted Nick at his UK office and spoke with him at length.

"They laughed because they all knew they would never have achieved the task so well if someone had tried to lead or manage the process," he confirms. "It was a highly complex exercise which was done quickly without a nominated leader. Indeed, if it had been given an assigned leader, it would take far longer and probably not succeed at all. Yet many leaders try to do just that—overcontrol and overregulate their organizations—because they mistakenly think that what they see in black and white on an organizational chart depicts reality. The world simply doesn't work like that! It's dominated by interrelationships, paradox, self-organizing and emergent properties."

In other words, the traditional practice of leadership attempts to do exactly what traditional traffic controls attempt to do, with the leader acting as chief traffic cop.

"As Lao Tzu wrote," concludes Nick, "'a leader is best when people barely know he exists; when his work is done, his aim fulfilled, they will say: we did it ourselves.'"

IT'S ONLY NATURAL

The reason the simplest rules create the most effective experience is that the universe is governed by simple rules. Yet in our false belief that we have better answers, we violate those rules repeatedly, nearly always to our detriment. Brilliant thinkers over the course of history have devoted their lives to understanding and explaining how nature works. Ignoring that information stifles our creativity and stunts our effectiveness; exploiting it can be incredibly powerful.

There is a Zen aesthetic principle known as *shizen*, meaning "naturalness." The goal of using *shizen* is to strike a balance between being "of nature" and being distinct from it—to be viewed as being without pretense, without artifice, unforced, yet to be revealed as intentional rather than accidental or haphazard.

Shared space is an example of *shizen*.

My point is simply this: whatever problem you're trying to solve, look first for naturally occurring patterns and rhythms. If you don't see them at first, strip away the obvious things that might be obscuring them, as Ben Hamilton-Baillie does in his design of a shared space. Then incorporate them into your solution.

The second law of subtraction is natural. We need to keep that in mind when we are creating, designing, or building anything.

SILHOUETTES

IN SUBTRACTION

William C. Taylor

Brad Smith

Khoi Vinh

John Shook

Bob Harrison

Nick Obolensky

Dan Markovitz

John Hunter

Seth Kahan

FRINGE RULES

William C. Taylor

We tend to make things more complicated than they need to be. If we want to do something big, if we want to create something important, if we want to design something impressive, we impose detailed rules, assign endless tasks, and empanel a bureaucracy to monitor progress. That's just the way the world works, right? Wrong. A few simple design principles, well crafted and deeply felt, can unleash remarkable waves of creativity.

Every August since 1947, Edinburgh, Scotland, has played host to the renowned three-week-long Edinburgh Festival Fringe. It is the largest arts gathering in the world, offering nearly 42,000 performances of 2,542 shows hosted by 258 venues and featuring 21,192 performers.

It's also a compelling case of how unchecked human energy, shaped by a few simple rules, can unleash truly amazing results.

Here's the thing: *No one is in charge of the Fringe.* The festival's small staff doesn't decide who performs or where and doesn't influence the overall mix of performances. There is no artistic guru, no committee, no guiding body of any kind. Yet an extraordinary cluster of performers turns up every year to move the mix in a new direction.

So what makes the Fringe work? Participation and creativity, blended with a spirit of competition. The Fringe is self-organizing, governed by the self-interest of the performers, the venues, the audience, and the press. Anyone is eligible to perform; all you have to do is to persuade one of the 250-plus venues to host your show. Then you persuade visitors to attend your show instead of the hundreds of others taking place at the same time and persuade critics to review your show. That's it. In other words, it's the participants—artists and audience—who are "in charge."

Want to make your organization more competitive? Maximize opportunities for people to collaborate with many smart people outside your organization, encourage participants to compete with one another, and minimize the natural leadership instinct to control the interactions.

The job of Fringe staff is to do the minimum necessary to make the event happen. As artistic director Paul Gudgin told me: "The *worst* thing we could do is to decide what kind of festival Edinburgh should be, to engage in what I call programming through the back door. My most important responsibility is to make sure that the people who decide what the festival should be are the artists and the audience. What we have to do at all times is to make as few rules as possible."

William Taylor is a founding editor of Fast Company *and the bestselling author of* Practically Radical, *from which he adapted this story.*

THE TWO-PIZZA RULE

Brad Smith

Innovation is at the core of all we do. We work hard to make sure our developers have both the freedom and the focus they need to succeed. As we've grown and expanded over the years, we've learned that when it comes to building a culture of innovation, less is often best.

Size and scope are not always the key to success. In fact, often those two things work against you. Employees can lose focus, and good ideas can have trouble finding the light of day, and even when they do, they can get shot down by the bottleneck of leadership and conventional company wisdom.

That's why we've taken a subtractive approach to innovation. We've developed lean and simple structures to remove many of the barriers that can sometimes hold good ideas and individuals back.

We start with our Two-Pizza Rule, which is that our development teams can be no larger than the number of people who can be fed by two pizzas. Keeping the teams small allows the members to stay nimble and make decisions quickly.

Then we make sure these teams have a clear and specific vision. If you try to solve too many problems, you end up solving none. We ensure that our small teams are tightly focused on a specific, real-world customer need. By keeping the project scope narrow and specific, we create a laserlike focus that spurs innovative products and services with real and enduring value.

And then, in the spirit of simplicity, we encourage our teams to develop a minimum viable product and get it into the hands of customers as quickly as possible: our developers put a working prototype together, and rather than try and improve it based on their own opinions, we bring our customers into the development process. Instead of trying to solve everything the first time around, we emphasize speedy execution and constant experimentation. We get the customer feedback and rapidly iterate until we create a product that truly delights and improves the lives of our customers. Ultimately it helps us grow.

Keeping it simple isn't easy. The bigger you are, the harder it is. You need clear focus and strong discipline. By exploiting subtraction in innovation, we've been able to create an environment of freedom and creativity that allows us to thrive and grow.

Brad Smith is the president and chief executive officer of Intuit, which is consistently ranked as one of the most admired tech companies and best places to work.

THE ART OF SUBTRACTION

Khoi Vinh

Something interesting happened after the iPad debuted and quickly became ubiquitous. Suddenly people with little or no confirmed artistic talent were bringing home a perfect digital art-making tool. Many software developers seemed to recognize this too, and dozens of art apps started appearing.

You would think that this confluence of market, device, and software would produce plenty of new amateur artists, but that didn't happen. Art apps were popular, but most people tried them just once or twice before abandoning them.

Why was that? Because the art apps were powerful re-creations of real-world art-making tools, but none of them were social. They didn't challenge the old idea that creating art is a solitary act. For most people who don't think of themselves as artists, it's difficult to muster the motivation to keep plugging away at art if the core experience remains a lonely one.

A social art experience could change everything. It could allow millions of iPad consumers to make art—and have fun doing it—before they even realized it was art.

That was the inspiration behind Mixel, the social collage app for the iPad that my business partner and I launched in November 2011. But as we built Mixel, we realized something else: All the art apps had failed to inspire amateurs because they were *too* powerful. The apps were simply iPad versions of desktop tools that were complicated and feature-heavy.

We knew early on that Mixel wouldn't be able to match such power, and so the actual tools that we built for creating art were purposefully basic, spare, inexact, and even primitive. We saw something interesting in early testing that informed our attitude toward creative tools: imprecision is liberating. No one using Mixel's simple tools ever felt that he or she was doing something wrong. The tool is so rough and inexact that people believe there's really no getting it wrong.

This profound insight helped us make something unique. Instead of striving to create a full arsenal of tools, we looked for opportunities where strategic omissions and imposed limitations would free users and unlock their creativity. This let them off the hook for creating "great masterworks" and let them settle into the more comfortable and engaging territory of releasing their creative energies into collages made in minutes, not hours.

The result has been a teeming community of amateur artists pouring their creative souls into a nearly limitless array of visual self-expressions that never would have happened with more powerful and precise software.

Khoi Vinh (subtraction.com) is a cofounder of the iPad app Mixel and a former design director for the New York Times Magazine.

SLEEPLESS IN SUBTRACTION

John Shook

I participated in my first three-day zero-sleep *kaizen* workshop in a machining welding cell in the mid-1980s at Toyota's Motomachi plant in Toyota City. The way these *kaizen* events work is that you start out by observing the actual conditions of the operation. It takes you most of an eight-hour shift to confirm what is happening at each job or machine under different conditions. After a quick dinner, you have to confirm what's going on during the night shift, which takes most of the shift as well.

Then it's time for the fun part—thinking of a better way: how to make the work easier for the worker, how to eliminate some waste such as excess inventory, or how to fix a recurring quality problem. Most ideas at this stage flow very easily and directly from the detailed observations you've documented. This part is always the most fun and fulfilling.

Next is the hard part: testing out your ideas and changes without screwing things up for the workers. Of course, none of the ideas work quite right. Sometimes the workers can tell you right away, "No, that won't work." This trial and error, sometimes well-constructed experiments—but just as often simply "that didn't work, let's try this"—continues through day and night two. There is no sleep: none, zero, zip. When dawn came on day three, I was exhausted. My sensei for the event had been both relentlessness and patient throughout.

We were focused on increasing production: how to get more product out. Inability to meet requirements without overtime was blowing the budget as well as spirits, especially since we knew more was on its way. We'd be working more overtime if we couldn't come up with real improvements.

But with no sleep and our deadline approaching, my sensei was totally dissatisfied with most of our ideas. Finally he asked, "Why do you keep trying to push for more when all you have to do is remove what's in the way?"

That got our attention. "Look at all the extra walking," he said. "Can't you eliminate it? Look at all the lifting of that heavy inventory. Can't you take it away? Look at all the waiting. Can't you remove the blockages so things will flow smoothly?" Then the kicker: "You really can accomplish more for the workers by asking them to do less."

When it was all over, I asked my sensei why he didn't tell us that from the beginning. "I did not tell you anything," he replied. "I simply removed a blockage from your mind. And I could not remove that blockage until it was in the way."

John Shook is the chairman and CEO of the Lean Enterprise Institute and the author of several books, including Learning to See *and* Managing to Learn.

UNSTUCK IN TRAFFIC

Bob Harrison

 In 1991, I was a police lieutenant for the City of Coronado, California, recently assigned as the department's patrol division commander. Coronado is located on a peninsula facing the Pacific Ocean, just across the Coronado Bay Bridge from San Diego. It's a unique locale, home to the aircraft carriers of the Navy's Pacific Fleet and the Hotel Del Coronado, where Frank Baum penned *Dorothy and the Wizard of Oz* in 1908.

Every July Fourth, Coronado displays its fireworks show at 9:00 p.m., coinciding with San Diego's fireworks show across the bay. A significant number of the 350,000 people who view these shows annually do so from Coronado's shores. The entire Coronado Police Department, all 45 officers, is fully deployed to manage all the goings-on. When the fireworks conclude at about nine-thirty, it is nothing short of gridlock for the next two hours as visitors leave town.

Like almost any other police agency facing these crowds, Coronado's officers were traditionally stationed at key intersections, traffic signals were placed on red flash, and the police actively directed departing traffic along one of two major routes. The work was tiring, noisy, and dangerous; accidents occurred, cars stalled, and the duty was among the least favored for any officer assigned.

I thought there must be a more effective way to help clear the city of congestion at the day's end. In a meeting with traffic personnel, someone suggested tongue-in-cheek that we should just "go home early" to avoid the crowds. That's when the idea struck: why not? What if we didn't direct traffic? What if we just monitored it instead and worked to clear the roadways as needed while relying on the individual drivers to move through the city in reasonable ways?

On July 4, 1991, we did it. Officers were present at key intersections but did not direct traffic. At the night's end, we were surprised, pleased, and more than a little amused that what took about 90 minutes the previous year took almost exactly the same amount of time this year. We repeated the "unplan" the next year. Same results. In fact, in 1993, we pulled officers back even farther, to monitor but not be readily visible, and the time actually decreased by another five minutes.

The unplan is still used to this day. Sometimes doing nothing is the best thing you can do.

Bob Harrison is a retired chief of police and manages the California POST Command College, an intensive executive development program for aspiring chiefs of police.

KISS

Nick Obolensky

In my work, I use a version of KISS, one other than "Keep It Simple, Stupid" or "Keep It Short and Simple." It's "Keep, Increase, Start, and Stop."

Many of the executives I work with are spending half their time doing stuff that just isn't important when I first introduce them to KISS. The "Stops" are the hardest to identify—we all like to think what we are doing is important—but in fact they often render the best results. These stops can be at the individual, team, or organizational level. They may seem small, but like the butterfly effect, they often achieve a disproportionately positive result.

I remember in particular a pharmaceutical company I worked with that eliminated its onerous expense policy and replaced it with a simple rule: people could sign off their own expenses but had to post them on an intranet website designed just for that purpose.

In other words, they made expenses completely transparent to everyone. Expenses went down and cost and time savings went up as people shared best deals and challenged one another when they saw expenses being too high. A wonderful self-regulating system emerged.

My favorite story, though, is about an insurance company where a busy marketing executive was invited (read, ordered) by the CEO to join a change team for one day per week. The invitation made him angry for some reason.

I met him some time later and asked him how things were going given his initial reaction. He revealed to me why he had been so angry: he had gone back to his office after the meeting in which the CEO had invited him to be on the team and called in his assistant, and they had gone through his diary, removing some of the work he did and meetings he usually attended in order to free up one day each week.

I didn't get it. What made him so angry?

His reply: "Nobody noticed."

Nick Obolensky (complexadaptiveleadership.com) is a UK-based leadership development consultant and the author of Complex Adaptive Leadership.

FAIR GAME

Dan Markovitz

Several years ago, I managed a team of seven people.

Our company had a fairly typical HR [human resources] handbook filled with rules and regulations covering everything in mind-numbing detail: how many vacation days you got, how they would be accrued, and when they could be taken.

Managing vacation requests was a hassle. People had to submit vacation requests to me, and I had to forward them to HR. The process was a huge time suck for everyone. We had more important work to do. And we couldn't always fill out the forms in advance, as required. As product marketers, we traveled extensively, which made it difficult to fill out and file the required forms in advance.

I decided the best way to handle this vacation request issue was to simply ignore it.

I told my team that as long as they got their jobs done, I didn't care how many vacation days they took each year. After all, if they could satisfactorily fulfill their job responsibilities while taking three or four weeks off per year, more power to them!

I told them that I trusted their judgment on what they felt was an appropriate number of days off to take each year. I figured if the company could trust them enough to manage the product line, I could certainly trust them to manage their own vacation time. My only requirement was that they had to check with me before taking time off to ensure that they wouldn't be out right before some critical deadline.

It worked. I was freed from paper shuffling, my team felt respected, and they took the vacation time they needed to refresh and recover from their travel. And most interestingly, the number of vacation days they took actually *decreased*.

It took me a while to figure it out, but really it makes perfect sense: when you're told you only have 10 days off, immediately you try to figure out how to get 11 days—you chafe at the restrictions, and you want to game the system. But when you're told you can take as many days off as you want as long as you use your best judgment and don't abuse the privilege—well, that's the heaviest burden of all.

My team's focus shifted from figuring how to beat the system to figuring out how to live up to the responsibility placed upon them.

And they did it—beautifully.

Dan Markovitz (timebackmanagement.com) is the founder of TimeBack Management, a faculty member at the Lean Enterprise Institute, and the author of A Factory of One.

MANAGE LESS, MANAGE BETTER

John Hunter

Early in my career, I had a supervisor ask me why I wasn't working. I was away from my desk—not reading, not typing on my keyboard, not talking on the phone, not in a meeting, staring off into space, apparently just wasting time. I explained that I was thinking.

The busier we are, the more productive we are. Or so many managers think. It can be tempting to cram your days full of activity to show how hardworking and vital you are. Finding time to think is hard enough; maxing out your capacity makes it next to impossible.

Everyone agrees taking time to think is wise. But I have rarely seen managers make it a priority. Managers will say they value it, but they cram schedules so full that they can't really spend time thinking. Result: people are busy just being busy.

I never forgot that early lesson when I became a manager of a software development team. Software programmers seem to understand the importance of thinking. One of the secrets to successful programming is that it takes deep, uninterrupted thought.

My main focus when managing my software development team was to let the team be. My most important task was to ensure that the developers had a clear vision of our business aims, what the priorities were, then get out of the way and give people uninterrupted time to do their work.

Most of what I needed to do simply required listening, observing, thinking, and sometimes deciding. Action wasn't high on the list. My goal was to intervene as little as possible, and then only when doing so would optimize the whole system.

I wanted to make sure the developers had an environment that allowed them to succeed: the resources they needed, the time they needed, coaching when they needed it, freedom from unreasonable demands, the opportunity to take risks, and protection when something didn't work.

Still, I stepped in more than I wanted to. I'm still learning. And by managing even less, I know I'll become more effective.

Act less, and act well when you do. You'll make things better for everyone.

John Hunter (johnhunter.com) is the founder and CEO of Curious Cat Ltd. (management.curiouscat-blog.net) and the author of Management Matters. *He currently lives and works in Malaysia.*

A LITTLE LESS MORE

Seth Kahan

Years ago I worked for the World Bank. They wanted to provide a global knowledge management system, which was all the rage in the 1990s.

The first effort was a kitchen sink solution: a big, bloated version of a private online encyclopedia, a catalog of every document, spreadsheet, and presentation the organization owned, all of which were to be dumped into the online storage facility to be "easily" accessed by staff members.

The whole effort was a bust. Even after a Herculean collection and cataloging effort, the vast majority of entries remained empty. When people ventured in to see what was there, they mostly found nothing. One or two experiences like that was all it took and they'd had it. They left and didn't come back.

The technology leadership team didn't get it and kept building the ultimate knowledge store. Finally my boss created a color-coded visual map showing how many of the categories were simply empty. Then they got it. Question was: What to do?

There was one bright spot, a little tool that provided people with two bits of information: a country-specific news feed coupled with a weather forecaster. It was considered a cool little gadget and not very important. But it was a major hit in terms of usage. It brought people to the site in droves. Travel was a regular part of organizational life at the World Bank. The ability to quickly and effortlessly find these two important things was immensely useful. It informed people what was going on at their destination and what clothes to pack.

That tiny, dirt-simple little tool saved the entire knowledge management system.

It was a huge aha moment. Instead of seeing the technology and its massive storage as the centerpiece, we shifted our focus to the people and creating quality interactions. We put our efforts into convening special events that brought people together to think about key issues or otherwise interact in helpful ways.

It dawned on us that it wasn't about knowledge storage but knowledge creation. We put together a knowledge fair. We built thematic groups organized around important topics. Instead of trying to build a virtual Library of Congress, we focused on learning how to bring people together in productive ways.

Most of those groups still exist 10 years later. These groups have survived reorganizations, budget swings, even leadership changes.

Attempting to be comprehensive is sometimes the enemy of utility.

Seth Kahan (sethkahan.com) is the bestselling author of Getting Change Right.

LAW NO. 3

LIMITING INFORMATION

ENGAGES

THE IMAGINATION

A true work of art is one whose imperfect beauty makes an artist of the viewer.
Soetsu Yanagi

A pple used it in launching the original iPhone in 2007 as well as in its entertaining "I'm a Mac" commercials. David Chase used it in the groundbreaking final episode of *The Sopranos*. Cadbury used it in its "In the Air" commercial, which went viral on YouTube. Hollywood uses it all the time in movie trailers. Agatha Christie was the undisputed heavyweight champion of it. Mike Nichols used it in the famous underwater pool scene in *The Graduate*. Screenwriter and director J. J. Abrams has built a phenomenal career around it. In-N-Out Burger uses it with its menu. Sudoku relies on it, as do comic books, crossword puzzles, and text messaging. Leonardo da Vinci used it to paint the *Mona Lisa*, and Paul Cezanne became known for it. *The New Yorker* exploits it for its popular cartoon caption contest. The Japanese poet Fujiwara no Teika believed it to be at the heart of true art. And long before all of them, ancient Chinese gardens were designed around it. And I'm using it to write this paragraph.

With any luck, that first paragraph raised a question in your mind about the "it." In case you haven't figured it out from my admittedly clumsy clues, the it is incomplete information. Zen artists call it *yugen*, which means "subtlety," and it is the focus of the third law of subtraction: *Limiting information engages the imagination.*

Artfully incomplete or limited information creates intrigue, piques curiosity, heightens anticipation, and triggers our fascination through what my friend Sally Hogshead labels mystique. Sally knows a thing or two about fascination, having written a bestselling book called *Fascinate*. Here's Sally on mystique:

> Eye-catching enough to get noticed, yet complex enough to stay interesting. Revealing enough to pique curiosity, yet shadowy enough to prompt questions. Mystique flirts with us, provoking our imagination, hinting at the possibilities, inviting us to move closer while eluding our grasp. It doles out information, without ever actually giving anything away. . . . [T]his trigger is rooted in unfulfillment . . . is the most nuanced and perhaps most difficult to achieve. Mystique invites others closer without giving them what they seek. A delicate

balance to be sure, but successfully achieved, it's fascination's exemplar. Mystique can add anticipation and curiosity to any relationship, from new business pitches to social invitations, by motivating others to return for more.

Well said. And with that fine prologue, allow me to introduce you to a modern master of mystique whose work fascinates over 2 million people each and every day.

CONNECTING THE DOTS

You don't need to see the masthead to know that the person four rows ahead of you on the airplane is reading the *Wall Street Journal*. You can tell at a glance. It has nothing to do with the paper—you can tell even if someone is reading it on an iPad—and there's nothing truly unique about the page layout. All you need to do is catch a glimpse of one of those tiny, fascinating, yet minimal portraits of someone prominent. You know the ones I'm talking about: countless little dots only, yet utterly photorealistic. You can't help but marvel at them. The *Wall Street Journal*'s portrait style has become its trademark. It's called a hedcut,* and it was Kevin Sprouls who created it in 1979.

Here's Kevin, by his own hand:

*Hed *is a journalist's slang for "headline," and cut refers to the 600-year-old art of the woodcut, which is an essentially subtractive printing technique akin to the etching portraiture style used on U.S. currency. It is more formally known as xylography and involves working in relief, like sculpting: material is removed from a block to create the white or negative, nonprinting part of the illustration. The printing parts are those which remain on the surface of the block. The dot-art technique used in hedcuts is called stippling, which also is known in the art world as pointillism.*

I am sure you realize by now that what you see is not really there, that you're looking at an advanced handcrafted optical illusion. All that's really there, of course, are dots and white space, and it is the art of the space between the carefully placed dots that engages your brain to recall patterns and participate in the act of rendering the final image. Kevin achieves an enormous level of detail through minimal means by making you an active collaborator and exploiting the gestalt principle of *closure*, which is your brain's way of mentally completing that which is incomplete, using patterns grooved from past experience. (I'll say more about closure in the second half of this chapter.)

Kevin also prompts you to wonder: How do they do that? He makes you work just hard enough that you're aware that there is something different and unique here, that it's not a photograph (which you wouldn't look twice at) but something more interesting so that you lean forward for a closer look. "Leaning forward" is the first goal in attracting others to whatever it is you're offering. The longer they lean forward, the longer they remain engaged, which is the ultimate goal of crafting any experience.

Kevin has kept people leaning forward for over 30 years. He trained the artists who carry on the style he created at the *Journal*, keeping the tradition alive long after he moved on to broaden his illustrative horizons. His work has been featured in *Smithsonian* magazine, and his pen is housed in the Newseum in Washington, D.C. Thousands of people all over the world have tried to copy and computerize his craft, to no avail. His art can only be done painstakingly by hand.

I contacted Kevin and spent a good bit of time chatting with him to understand his methodology, because his iconic style is a good metaphor for the way limited information can be used to create clarity far more compelling and indelible in the viewer's mind than something perfectly concrete and complete.

"It began when I was in high school," Kevin tells me. "I think I was around fifteen at the time. I had this friend, a bit older than me, who worked in an architect's office. He left that job, but he took this set of brand new Koh-I-Noor Rapidograph pens. They're these technical pens with a really fine point. He knew I was big into art and drawing, so he gave them to me. I started playing around with them. I could make these precise little marks. They lend themselves to detail, the pointillistic or 'stipple' technique. I basically taught myself, and I learned how to produce subtle tonal variations with minimal marks, dots, and lines. I loved the precision of it. I've been at it ever since. I brought those pens with me to art school. I was doing all kinds of drawings with those stupid things. In art school, my attraction to drawing with pens found me using the stipple technique in etchings and illustration assignments. Lines and etchings are actually much harder than dots, so art school really made me better."

Kevin attended Temple University's Tyler School of Art in Philadelphia, all along continuing to hone his pointillist prowess. In his final year, he spent a semester in Rome, studying printmaking and sculpture. Perhaps not surprisingly, Kevin fell in love with bronze casting, clay modeling, and sculpture, discovering that he had flair for modeling from life. After graduation in 1977, he landed a freelance gig at Dow Jones & Company, parent to the *Wall Street Journal*.

"I got called to New York to talk to the art director," Kevin recalls. "My roommate from art school referred me, and I ended up spending two years freelancing for the marketing department on the fourth floor of 22 Cortlandt Street learning the newspaper business and doing some fairly routine advertising stuff, lots of mechanicals and graphic design. I remember I played around a lot with letter spacing and typesetting, especially with the hot new typeface at the time, called Helvetica. The cafeteria was one floor up, and the *Journal* editors and reporters were above that on six. We all read the *Journal* as part of the job, and I got to know people there just by hanging out in the cafeteria."

At that time, the *Wall Street Journal* did not use photographs except in advertisements and used very few illustrated portraits. "The *Journal* was famous for having no pictures," explains Kevin. "The one exception was when they used a photograph to show Ted Kennedy's route during the Chappaquiddick incident. They had a guy I think in South Carolina doing the portraits. Hedcuts, they called them. He was using soft pencil on coquille board, which is a pebbled surface. One day in the cafeteria, I asked the page one editor, Glynn Mapes, to try me out on a portrait, knowing I could give him something good. I really wanted to do illustration rather than the graphic work I was then engaged in. He said yes, probably out of convenience more than anything. I really just happened to be the right guy at the right time, in the right place. Still, they hired me to do some portraits, and I started developing a new style. I pulled out my trusty pens and started experimenting. It took me quite a while, mostly because of the technology of the printing press back then. When I started out, I was paid $75 per drawing. Eventually, they dropped the previous artist and began using me exclusively. Eventually, they hired me full-time, and I began to train other artists we deemed had the talent, skill, and, really, discipline—it takes six to eight hours to do one of these."

In some of those early experiments, Kevin included lines with the dots. The challenge was getting the hair and clothing just right. After several iterations over the course of several months, his current style—dots only—came into focus. "It took a lot of experimenting," he explained to me. "I finally figured out that if I drew the image at a larger size of three inches by five inches and reduced it to a third of the size to fit the half-column width, which at the time was seven and a half picas, dialed down the camera exposure—I was always fighting with the camera guys who wanted to overexpose everything, which kills detail—I could achieve just the right contrast that gives it that three-dimensional quality. I could get the impact and nuance and subtlety I was after."

I asked Kevin why he thought the portraits still hold such fascination for people in light of all the advanced multimedia technology used currently to produce the *Journal*. "I think the technique is successful in the *Journal* because it comes off as engraving work, as in stock certificates, as in currency. It is very small, but people still remark on the art of it, even as the *Journal* of today is quite a splashy visual affair. I think the drawings are perceived as things of quality, things well made, like fine jewelry. The detail, and the small scale, and probably the uniqueness of being a piece of black-and-white line art that renders a unique photoreal image invite curiosity and closer inspection. These factors differentiate this art form from all the other glaring distractions in the paper—the full-color, large-scale photography, advertising, etcetera etcetera."

Kevin left the *Journal* in 1987 to head for the Pine Barrens of New Jersey, where he spends his winter days hunched over a drafting table overlooking a lagoon, dotting away. He splits his time between there and Long

Beach Island, where he has a summer bungalow. "My day starts around ten in the morning, and I go through to about eleven at night," he tells me. "This stuff takes a long time!"

The Revealing

So just how does the process unfold? I was more than curious, so I asked Kevin if he wouldn't mind walking me through the key stages, with me as the subject.

It all begins with a good photograph. "I ask for something that is clear, in focus, with enough detail to work with in terms of highs and lows, contrast," says Kevin. "Many of my clients send photos to work with that, I must say, can be challenging. They're too small, low resolution, or a studio shot with direct light that washes out highlights, lowlights, shadows, and, really, the things that make a person real. The best shots are simple, shot with a good camera using natural light. I ask people to just go stand by a window and have someone take their picture. It's more authentic than studio posing."

Kevin's arsenal of equipment is minimal: draftsman's lead holder with HB lead, kneaded rubber eraser, Rapidograph pens, supply of ink, fine high-quality paintbrush and some white designer's gouache to take care of any "adjustments" that might be necessary, tracing paper, illustration board, scanner, computer, and Adobe Photoshop software. The first step is to scan the photo, get it into Photoshop, and convert it to grayscale and then adjust certain levels, size it, and crop it.

"I print out the grayscale image and transfer the photo's information onto illustration board by tracing on the photo," Kevin explains. "The resulting contour drawing is like a map for me to follow. Everything is done by hand, one mark of the pen at a time."

He then begins the step-by-step incremental process of placing dots meticulously on the illustration board. Clothing, hair, and eyes are the most challenging, and so Kevin focuses his attention there first. "Get that framework right," he says, "and the rest is a matter of, um, connecting the dots." On the next few pages you can see how he does just that.

"What constitutes a good-quality portrait in this style is the structure of the dot field," Kevin tells me. "To produce that tonal effect, I align the marks into a grid matrix. All of us dotters, or stipple artists, have different looks and levels of quality. I understand that the *Journal* folks nowadays draw on thin paper over light boxes to produce their finished works. Something I would never do! My standard process is to trace the image onto the board, then ink it, while constantly referring to the photographic image."

Here is the finished product, revealed after about six hours of hard work. If the portrait were going in the *Wall Street Journal* (unlikely in my case), this image would be reduced to roughly a third of the drawn size to fit into the newspaper column, which is about an inch wide. I've put the photograph and the hedcut side by side below. Ignoring the subject for a moment, which one is more interesting? Which one makes you want to lean in and take a closer look? Which one engages your brain more?

I find several things about this exercise instructive. If you're able to make the mental leap of abstraction to see how it might apply to your unique challenge, I believe that what you'll find below the surface is a subtractive creative approach that is indeed universally applicable in using minimum means to produce maximum effect.

It begins with the prestep of getting the starting point just right. Getting the proper starting image is the key; you need one with enough vivid detail to enable a clear endgame to be visualized. Too often in life it isn't. People don't recognize success because they don't know what it looks like. There's a reason everyone talks about the big picture. It's difficult to remain fully engaged without that bigger picture, because our daily work is really about putting a little dot down each day, metaphorically speaking. Something needs to guide us in connecting them. If we are missing the mark, so to speak, we can usually trace it to a glaring absence of a compelling mental image to guide the effort. Pictures connect the right brain with the left and help us see the path more clearly.

The second item entails the actual construction of the new picture. When you're creating a new reality, a good bit of the old one gets destroyed. But some things don't change. In Kevin's process, nearly all the detail of the starting image is removed: all but the outline and contours that define the person. In business, work, and life, that framework is often a combination of core values and purpose in life. The manner in which the ultimate vision is achieved and the way the endgame is rendered stylistically always change. That's the creative part. What doesn't change are the very things that define who we are: what we stand for, why we exist.

A third lesson concerns the discipline and incrementality of the work. If you scan the web, you'll find many people who have tried and failed to reproduce Kevin's craft in ways that shortcut the talent, skill, and painstaking effort required to produce his art. They are trying to eliminate the wrong thing: tradecraft. They want the final result in one big swag with the punch of a few computer keys. They want someone or some*thing* to do the work for them. They want the breakthrough effect without the hard work that goes with it. Too often we seek the grand-slam home run and forgo the ground ball single that gets us on base. Creativity and innovation in any field is a matter of increments. Ultimately, all the small steps reveal something altogether new and novel. Too often in work and life we force what amounts to a false choice between small steps and big leaps. It isn't about choosing one or the other. It's about achieving big leaps *through* small steps. Kevin's work is a systematic pursuit dedicated to achieving the maximum effect with the minimum means. If everyone took his basic creative approach, we wouldn't be dealing with so much excess everything.

The final thing I took away from the project concerns technique. I asked Kevin if he squints a lot. I asked him in all seriousness. In his book *The Laws of Simplicity*, John Maeda mentioned "the squint":

> The best designers in the world all squint when they look at something. They squint to see the forest from the trees—to find the right balance. Squint at the world. You will see more, by seeing less.

I began using and developing my ability to do the squint after reading that. The squint has become a go-to technique in nearly everything I attempt, no matter what the activity may be. Sometimes it's a literal squint; sometimes it's a figurative one. For example, when I'm involved in developing strategy, it's a squint of sorts that helps me see the bigger picture; when I'm prioritizing goals and plans, it helps me focus; when I'm in the throes of execution—writing, speaking, coaching—it helps me create visual and verbal flow.

"Absolutely I squint, and I've got the wrinkles and reading glasses to prove it," Kevin jokes. "But seriously, yes. Squinting shows you what to pay attention to, what to ignore. It helps me know when and where to add something or leave well enough alone. This work, and I guess any work if you think about it, is a constant process of focusing and unfocusing my eyes, working up close and then standing back, little details and the big picture. Or it should be, anyway."

Few people have the artistic ability of Kevin Sprouls, yet everyone has the ability to connect the dots. In his 2012 book *Too Big to Know*, David Weinberger writes about how until the 2010 earthquake in Haiti, there were no street maps of Port-au-Prince. An organization called OpenStreetMap.org had satellite maps but the maps lacked street names in Port-au-Prince, which were sorely needed during the crisis. People from all over the world, predominantly expatriate Haitians, contributed the names so that the map filled up. The map was used by everyone from the U.S. Marines to the World Bank to the United Nations—people connected the dots and completed the picture, which sped up the rescue and relief efforts enormously.

SPOTLIGHT ON

CONNECTING THE DOTS

We can all get better at using limited information to create engagement and spark our imagination. That's where Ayesha-Mathews Wadhwa can help. Ayesha is the "chief pixel bender" of the San Francisco–based Pix-Ink, a design firm she founded to serve brand marketing to women. Her biography on the PixInkDesign.com site actually reads "Connecting the Dots."

"Over the course of my fifteen years in design," says Ayesha, "I've come to believe that in order to be creative, the one thing we absolutely must subtract is *judgment*. We must do that, because it gets in the way of imagination. We can do this only by recognizing and removing barriers to creativity."

Barriers to creativity fall into two groups, according to Ayesha: habits and blocks. "Life conditions us into developing habits," she explains. "Yes, they help us perform many of our daily activities, both personal and professional, and so become ingrained. James L. Adams, in his book *Conceptual Blockbusting*, identifies four blocks to creativity: perceptual blocks, emotional blocks, cultural/environmental blocks, and intellectual/expressive blocks. Combine habits and blocks and what you have is a formula for rigid thinking, or imagination that comes preset with judgment. Most of our formal education trains our judicial thinking, teaching us the 'one correct way' to solve a problem and to judge others' solutions. When you add that to the overwhelm of the information age we all live in, I believe there is a strong case to be made for how limiting information actually engages the imagination."

Ayesha put together an exercise especially for readers of *The Laws of Subtraction*, using a few simple illustrations to show how limiting information actually engages the imagination. "You're probably familiar with the connect-the-dots puzzles we all solved as children: essentially you get a bunch of dots with numbers attached to them and connect the numbers with lines to get a specific figure or shape or design, like this."

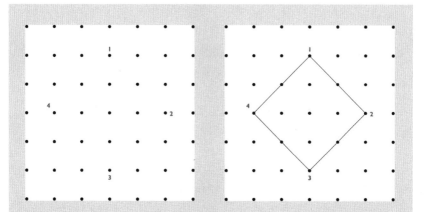

Connecting the above numbers 1 through 4 will lead to this shape: a diamond.

Great, problem solved! The mystery picture now reveals itself, and we feel validated that we've taken the information we've been given—the numbers—and connected the dots to create an intended form.

Now, what happens when you've been given these dots *without* numbers, as shown below: *information has been limited or removed altogether*. How does that invite your imagination to interact with these dots? This is where the fun really begins!

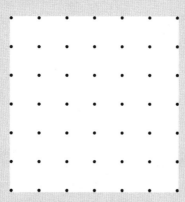

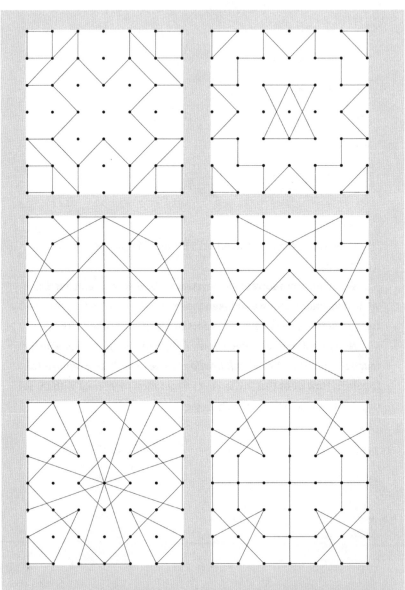

"In a span of 15 to 20 minutes, I generated a half dozen unique patterns or designs from the blank grid. If I kept going, I would most likely generate a dozen more, but the point of this exercise is to illustrate how limiting information engages the imagination. For me, this simple exercise reinforces Picasso's famous quote: 'To draw, you must close your eyes and sing.'"

IMAGINATION ENGAGED

On a typically warm southern California weekend in February, 20 of us are gathered at the Los Angeles Academy of Figurative Art for a two-day seminar called "Making Comics." I'm obviously not a cartoonist, but neither is half the class: there are teachers, engineers, architects, consultants, writers, editors, technologists, musicians, and one 14-year-old wunderkind of an aspiring graphic novelist. We all have at least three things in common: a desire to tell better stories, a fascination with imagination, and a love of imagery and visual thinking.

Each year nearly 150,000 people attend Comic-Con, the premier event for comics passionistas, manga mavens, anime auteurs, and graphic novel aficionados. The global market for comics of all types is huge; the art form is as old as the 3,200-year-old scenes painted on the tomb of Menna, the ancient Egyptian scribe. Hollywood's current trend toward producing film versions of comics has helped bring what has traditionally been the nerdy side of life into the mainstream. Comics encompass anything that contains images juxtaposed in a deliberate sequence to convey information and/or produce an aesthetic response in the viewer. In short, comics are sequential art.

"Imagination is the mortar that holds comics together," says the instructor, who is a staple feature at Comic-Con. "The true art is invisible." He should know, as his seminal 1993 graphic treatise on the subject, *Understanding Comics: The Invisible Art,* remains the definitive discourse on the theory and art of comics.

His name is Scott McCloud, and he had me at "imagination."

Three weeks earlier, I had spent the afternoon with Scott, and my interview with him had convinced me that I needed to experience further some of the things we discussed. He needed a break from the graphic novel he's furiously trying to complete by working 11 hours a day, and I wanted to know more about the magic of this "invisible art." I'm lucky: Scott and I live near each other, and unknown to us, his studio and my office had been in the same complex for years. Three days with Scott McCloud will turn your head around.

Visual Thinking

Scott McCloud wrote the popular *Zot!* comic book series from 1984 to 1991 before turning his attention to the theory of comics. The workshop I'm about to take is named after his 2006 book, *Making Comics: Storytelling Secrets of Comics, Manga and Graphic Novels*, which grew out of a longer course taught first at the Minneapolis College of Art and Design and later adopted by a number of colleges, including MIT. For the last half decade or so, Scott has been splitting his time between doing the work and teaching the craft. I ask him how he became interested in the theoretical side of comics.

"I was the son of an engineer," Scott tells me. "I looked at everything scientifically, which made cartooning a little hard. Things didn't come to me as intuitively as I'd have liked. After a while you can't fight your nature. It was organic. I just had a lot to say, lots of theories I wanted to tell people about. That's where *Understanding Comics* came from, and it only made sense to use the medium to make the book."

In 2008, Scott created a comic book for Google, explaining the inner workings of its then-new open source browser Google Chrome. The comic itself became an Internet phenomenon when it shipped ahead of the browser; for two days it was the only source of information about this major software release in the world. The *New York Times* said it was "akin to hiring Paul McCartney to write a jingle," while *Forbes* called it "one of the friendliest technical descriptions the software industry has yet produced."

You can see a sample on the next page.

"You do not need to know how to draw to be here today," Scott announces as the workshop gets under way. "This is about visual communication, visual storytelling, not drawing. But you will draw. In fact, I'm going to throw you in the deep end right away."

He does. We are given five minutes to draw this story: "A man is walking down the sidewalk, whistling. He meets an elephant. The elephant has a cell phone. The elephant hands the cell phone to the man. The man thanks the elephant and walks off a cliff."

The story is random for a reason. Scott wants to see how you tell a story you're not familiar with, one that has no context. "Draw, share, and critique are the three elements of this class," he explains. "And by critique I mean only did it communicate or not? No one has to say 'nice' or 'interesting' or anything like that, just 'is it a bicycle or an avocado?' and why did that communicate clearly or not?"

Scott asks us to stand up and form a circle, based on how many frames it took us to draw the elephant story, fewest to most. One person had drawn it in 4 panels, one person in 25, and the rest of us were somewhere in the middle. It took me five, one per story sentence.

"The number doesn't matter," Scott explains. "You could do it in two. You could do it in twenty. What matters is clarity, and clarity depends on the choices you make. You must make five key choices when showing and telling any story: choice of moment, choice of frame, choice of image, choice of word, and choice of flow. That's it."

Choice of moment is about deciding which moments to include in the story and which to leave out. "So much of creativity is editing," Scott says. "You can spew, but you have to edit. Pull out the long knives, folks. William Faulkner had it right when he said that in writing stories, you have to kill your darlings."

Choice of frame is about choosing the right distance and angle to view those moments and where to trim them. "For example," says Scott, "if you have your character full frame and facing out toward the reader, you've blocked your reader at the door. Have him turn slightly away and you invite the reader to step into the story."

Choice of images is about rendering the characters and objects and environments in those frames clearly, and choice of word is about picking words that add valuable information and work well with the images around them. Choice of flow is about guiding the audience through the story, between panels or pages or screens. "Those five decisions are the difference between clear and convincing storytelling and a big confusing mess," Scott informs us. "Today we are going to focus on the first three. No words today, friends."

That launches us into the next exercise, which will consume the rest of the day: we are each given a secret six-sentence story to draw. The stories were even more weird, nonlinear, and random than the elephant story. Everyone got something different, and we could not reveal the script. Scott gave us 20 minutes to draw the story in six panels or less, no words or even letters allowed.

Here's an example: "A businessman walks into a grocery store. The cashier waves hello. The man looks at the watermelons. A rhinoceros falls from the sky. The man puts it in his cart. He walks to the cashier and checks out."

Here's another: "A robot walks toward Big Ben. A person on a bicycle crashes into the robot. The robot's head falls off. It rolls away. A football player picks up the robot's head. He kicks it over Big Ben."

Yet another: "A mom takes her three children with her to the hardware store. Two of the children have a sword fight with rakes. The third child gets on a riding lawn mower while no one's looking and drives away. He leaves the store and drives onto the freeway. He drives to a speedway and enters the race. He wins the race on the lawn mower."

And one more: "A king walks into a hamburger joint. He orders a king-size hamburger. The hamburger is delivered to the king. The king puts his crown on the cashier. The king puts the hamburger on his head. Mark Twain drinks a toast."

The rest of the class then had to interpret and tell the story without any help from the artist. Only Scott knew the stories, which made the critique of each one immensely engaging and insightful. He was able to tease out the essential magic of comics. My story was the one about the robot (see page 88).

Life in the Gutter

The magic and mystery of comics, we learned, is not necessarily contained in the images or anywhere within the panels. It does not live in what is drawn. Rather, it is the gutter—the white space between the frames—that holds the secret. There is nothing in the space between, yet it's here where the real action occurs. It's here that the reader is drawn in. It's here that the reader is engaged, because it's here that the story is left open to interpretation. It's here that attention is focused, here that the imagination is sparked. And it's here that the real story takes place.

"The gutter invokes closure," Scott says. The gestalt principle of closure is something Scott spends a good bit of time on. He actually doesn't like the term, because there's too much pop psychology baggage around it. "I don't like 'gutter' either," he said to me during our interview. "I tried to change the language from panel and gutter to exposure and blink, but it didn't stick. At all."

Scott explains closure in terms everyone can understand. "At the heart of all comics is the phenomenon of observing the parts but perceiving the whole, of mentally completing that which is incomplete, based on past experience. We don't need every *t* crossed and *i* dotted. In our daily lives, closure allows us to make it through the day. I see the corner of a dollar bill peeking out of my wallet; I don't need to see the whole thing to know it's there. It's automatic."

In storytelling, though, it's a deliberate invention meant to engage audiences, Scott says. "It can take many forms, some simple, some complex; sometimes just a mere shape or outline is enough to trigger it." Scott draws a circle, then two smaller ones at ten o'clock and two o'clock. "What's this?" he asks. Mickey Mouse, of course. Anyone can see that.

During our interview, I mentioned the work of Kevin Sprouls. "Definitely closure," he says, nodding. "Our eyes take in the fragmented black and white of the patterns, and our brain transforms them into halftones, depth and dimension, and the reality of the face."

But for Scott, the visual perception described by closure is only half the story; it's the magic of the reader's experience produced by the space between that fascinates him, as it does me. "Whatever the mysteries within each panel, it's the power of closure *between* the panels that I find the most interesting. There's something strange and wonderful that happens in this blankness." He holds up his hands as if he's holding something in each: "The human imagination takes these two separate images, right? And there's not a single bit of information, not a single thing to see between them, but experience tells you something *must* be there and synthesizes something new, composes a single idea. Pure creativity; comics *is* closure!"

The closure in the comic medium is different from, say, the closure in film and television, which, like panels in a comic, goes frame by frame and moment by moment, but the increments and gaps are continuous and virtually imperceptible, thus largely involuntary. "Panels in comics fracture both time and space, offering a more jagged rhythm of unconnected moments," says Scott. "But closure allows us to connect these moments and mentally construct something unified and continuous. The difference is that the comic artist has a silent partner in crime: the reader. How you make the audience a willing and conscious collaborator, using closure as the agent of change, time, and motion—that's the invisible art."

One could even argue that the artist is innocent, simply the provocateur. "I can draw the raised axe, put a scream in the next frame," Scott writes in *Understanding Comics.* "But I'm not the one who let it fall, decided how hard the blow, or who screamed, or why. That's the special crime of the reader, each committing it in their own personal style. Each participated in the murder. Each held the axe and chose their spot. To kill a man between the panels is to condemn him to a thousand deaths."

In class, Scott discusses how participation is a powerful force in any medium. "Filmmakers realized that long ago," he tells us. "Intervals, silences, unexplained moments, unvoiced thoughts; all these things allow the audience to participate, to have their own interpretation. There's this silent agreement, a conspiracy, really, between the artists and their audience. Now, how any one artist honors that is a matter of craft."

"You've got to let any story breathe," Scott explained to me over lunch, weeks before the workshop. "It's like inhaling every once in a while. If I'm trying to nail down every concept in a literal fashion, it just doesn't breathe. You can easily suffocate your audience, drown them in a sea of too much information. You need those moments where the audience steps in. And it's the spaces, the silences, that create that rhythm."

At the mention of rhythm, I share with Scott my work with Toyota, my exposure to Japanese culture and the concept of *ma*. The discussion turns to differences in Eastern and Western storytelling. "Over there [in Japan] there's such a long and rich tradition of space in all their various art forms. Their style is much more an art of intervals, more than anywhere, really. The idea that elements omitted from a work of art are as much a part of that work as those included, that's been their specialty for literally hundreds of years. Here in the West, we don't wander much. We're so goal-oriented. Our bias for action is our thumbprint. In Japanese comics, you have that Zen thing happening. It's more about *being* there versus *getting* there. The Japanese use a lot more genuine silence. Silent panels. You know what's really funny? They have a sound effect for silence in comics. Maybe it's such a part of their culture that they think they need to make it overt."

I share with Scott my discussions with Lindon Leader, and he recognizes the name immediately. "In graphic arts you talk about negative space and figure–ground relationships." He nods. "Using minimal elements to master your art is a noble aspiration in any medium." When you listen to Scott talk, you realize he is a bit of a poet.

Back in class, Scotts uses the images on the next two pages, which he's allowed me to share, to tell us exactly what I wanted to hear: "Visual storytelling is as subtractive an art as it is additive. And finding the balance between too much and too little is crucial. To strike the right balance you have to make assumptions about audience experience. Some artists blow it. They assume way too much. You still have to manage the closure between the panels. If you're too ambiguous, too vague, there's nothing for the audience to go on. You need the Goldilocks touch: just enough, just right, and just in time."

Audience as Author

Expanding on the concept of just in time, Scott uses the metaphor of a trapeze artist, where you offer up information to the reader and then release the reader into the open air of imagination, only to be caught in the nick of time by the outstretched arms of the next panel. "Caught quickly so as not to let the reader fall into confusion or boredom," he says. "Or letting him free-fall without the wings to fly." Poetry.

At the end of the first day, we gather in a circle for some open "wondering about" discussion.

One student asks if there's a rule of thumb to help you manage your choices of moment. "If your reader is for some reason especially aware of the art in a given story," Scott replies, "then you might be making them work too hard. But it's also a matter of craft, style, and taste. The point is that all you can do is show the way. You can't take people somewhere they don't want to go. All you can do is make some good assumptions about the audience and hope you get them right. All you can do, really, is ask your audience for a little faith and a world of imagination."

I ask how we might go about developing that sensitivity to know better how and where to let the audience in. "Trial and error," answers Scott. "I wish I had a better or easier answer. You have to almost stand outside yourself. You have to become the audience, be the audience as you work. It's not easy. You have to capture, or recapture, the joy of reading if you're a writer, of viewing if you're a painter, of driving if you're designing cars. To put yourself in that state, to have that, I don't know, amnesia, where you're no longer a creator of the work, it's just something that arrives on your desk—someone else did it, and you can gauge your own reactions to it objectively."

As much for the other noncartoonist storytellers as for my own selfish purposes, I follow that up with a question about applying the concept of the gutter and audience participation in a nonliteral way to engage people's imaginations, for example, in an organization. "Well," Scott begins thoughtfully, "In organizations, leaders who are able to lead people to a conclusion without spelling it out are practicing something very much like that. If you think of the typical org chart where ideas flow from the top, that's the more didactic conception. If you have instead an organizational structure where there's inspiration that encourages the flow of ideas upward from the base, you might be looking at something more analogous to audience participation. More analogous to what we're trying to create with comics."

That seems to prompt another thought: "There's a compelling theory in video gaming about the secret to games—that games are about the abdication of authorship. What makes it a game, whether it's chess or *Super Mario Bros.* or *Grand Theft Auto,* is that the user feels as if they are the authors of their own experiences. There is a school of thought in gaming too of this notion of story and imposing stories upon games: with the story comes the author, and if there's a tension because the creator is trying to impose a story on the user, you begin to lose some of the character of what makes games games in the first place. But when the user feels empowered to create their own experience, they don't come away from the game talking about what someone made; they come away from that experience telling others 'what I did.' They're the star of that story. And it is the understanding of the nature of gaming that allows the gamer to create something more pure. It's that sense of user agency, that people create their own narratives. It's much more natural, much more organic, much more like a game from when you were playing on the playground as a kid."

What a great insight: the art of limiting information is really about letting people write their own story, which becomes much more engaging and powerful because they've invested their own intelligence and imagination and emotion.

"Look at Steve Jobs," Scott continues. "We saw the greatest control freak of all times in Jobs. But what was he doing ultimately? He was creating *nothing*. Take the iPad as an example. It's this empty vessel. It's a window. He was creating the means by which users could feel as if they were at the console of the universe. You know? But all of that design work, all of that control; he wasn't imposing control at all. He was handing the keys to us."

That may be the best explanation of why limiting information matters that I've ever heard. As creators, our job is to design the vehicle that allows drivers to go anywhere they desire.

Our assignment for the next day was perhaps the best and most instructive exercise in the art of subtraction I've encountered. Scott handed us a tabloid-size sheet of sketch paper with 16 panels on it, as you can see on the next page. Our challenge was to draw the narrative of our lives using only 16 moments to capture the essence of our story—no words, only images.

I encourage you to try it. It is one of the hardest things you'll ever attempt and one of the most subtractive. At the heart of the exercise are the three important decisions I introduced at the beginning of this book, and they are unavoidable in completing the exercise:

What to focus on and what to ignore

What to leave in and what to leave out

What to do and what to don't

It also sets the stage for a discussion of the fourth law of subtraction.

SILHOUETTES

IN SUBTRACTION

Don Norman

Helen Walters

Lisa Occhipinti

Markus Flanagan

Carmine Gallo

Sally Hogshead

Shawn Parr

Justin Brady

Mary Poppendieck

TOO MUCH INFORMATION

Don Norman

Our lives are complex. Our tasks are complex. Therefore, our tools must have a certain complexity to them. The question is, How should that be handled?

It's amazing how many people give a talk and want to tell others everything they know about a topic. They prepare a slide and want to tell all the important information that's on the slide. It becomes overwhelming.

When you're listening to a talk, you keep in mind only one or two critical points. So any good talk should only make one or two critical points.

Slides should be incredibly simple: one point and ideally no words, just images. I actually argue with Edward Tufte [*The Visual Display of Quantitative Information*] about this. He's very much against too little information on a slide. He doesn't agree with providing supplemental information that's not on the slide.

What I think Tufte misunderstands is the three different functions of a slide. One is to help the speaker. Many people need crutches to help remind themselves of what they want to say. If you need reminders, you should hide them from the audience. There's no reason the audience needs to see your crutch.

Second, there's what the audience sees on the slide. It should be simple, elegant, and easy to understand and shouldn't take away from their ability to listen to the speaker at the same time.

Finally, there's what they might want to take home and study later. And this is where Tufte is relevant. Tufte's slides are really great if you want to take them home and pore over them for 20 minutes. In the context of a talk, though, you don't have that 20 minutes to digest what you see and listen to the speaker at the same time.

Here's a case where utter simplicity is important in one situation but not in the other. Simplicity is context-sensitive.

Read John Maeda's book [*The Laws of Simplicity*]. It's short and appears not to have much information. It appears simple, but it's an incredibly complex book. John is a deep thinker and has this Zen master's way of writing. His law about "Subtract the obvious, add the meaningful" might be the sound of one hand clapping unless you understand the nuance of it. It's a simple statement but very deep. Subtraction is not just about what you want to take out or why; it's *how*.

Subtraction *requires* nuance. If you can unpack the nuance, that's a virtue—it's what people miss in the quest for simplicity.

Don Norman (jnd.org) is a cofounder of the Nielsen Norman Group and the author most recently of Living with Complexity.

THE SUBTRACTION OF WRITING

Helen Walters

The first time I saw Twitter being used in the wild was a strange experience. It was 2007. I sat next to a guy I knew in the auditorium of a conference and watched, confused, as he tapped into his laptop: "Sitting with Helen Walters from *BusinessWeek*." Why is that interesting? I asked him. "It's not, really," he answered, shrugging. So I gave him what I hoped was my most withering look and then turned my attention to the stage to focus on writing and reporting in the traditional way I had long understood.

Since then I've come to appreciate the 140-character medium. Twitter seems to embody the essence of subtraction. The brevity forces you to focus on what's truly important and to harness the restrictions as a challenge. The exercise of paring down meaning and insight into its purest form, formerly the purview of headline writers and the copy desk, is an invaluable one for anyone looking to communicate in the modern world. Such focused, clear thinking feeds back into the writing and thinking of a longer article, too.

In the years since I signed up for the service (in 2008, still reluctant, still grumpy, quickly addicted) I have marveled at the way in which this simple service has aided my writing, my thinking, my network, and my life. Many people seem to have constructed complex theories about the best ways to use it. My own philosophy aims to ape the simplicity of the service itself: don't overthink things. I tune in when I can; I write what I think; I engage with those I feel are real; I don't sweat the number of people following me; and I don't talk about what I had for lunch unless it was genuinely remarkable.

As the years have passed, the service has created new relationships, strengthened old ones, given me space to think aloud and to ask for feedback or critique. (And boy, do people deliver.) I have watched breaking news stories unfold; I have cried over updates from people I've never met; I've been guided to stories I would never have seen; and I've been introduced to incredible people I'd never have known were it not for this powerful yet brilliantly simple form of expression.

I know that many people still don't get Twitter, and there's certainly still time for the company to take a wrong turn, to pollute its purity with some bad business decisions. But for me, as a writer, I'm hugely grateful for the focus and clarity Twitter has afforded my life. #Thanks.

Helen Walters (thoughtyoushouldseethis.com) is a writer, innovation consultant with Doblin, and a former editor of innovation and design at Bloomberg Businessweek.

PERFECT BALANCE

Lisa Occhipinti

One of the first things you learn when studying visual art is the concept of positive and negative space and that they are equally important. In the same way, subtraction holds equal weight with addition. By removing, you strengthen, because the other elements are allowed to become clearer while whatever is subtracted leaves an imprint. Subtraction is not a taking away so much as a refining.

For example, in some of my paintings I include drawing. I will begin with a turbulent ground of color and texture, lay the drawing in, and then paint out around the edges of that drawn shape to allow it to come forward. I am subtracting negative space. Because I have defined and refined the background area, the drawn subject can effortlessly emerge. Just as easily, I might have thickened or darkened the drawing's outlines or filled it in with saturated color to make it more dominant, but the essence of that initial gesture of pencil to canvas would be lost, and so would its elegance.

Knowing what to leave out or take out is as crucial as knowing what to include. Subtraction is just as much an ingredient of constructing as addition is. When we begin a task, we naturally want the result to be perfect. This can lure us to include every morsel we think will produce an ideal outcome, but too often it is at the disservice of the larger intent and can detract from its dignity.

I think of subtraction as a recipe, and time is the oven temperature. Time clarifies by allowing the unessential to cook out so that you're left with a rich reduction. When I'm cornered by an undertaking, I cede it to time to gain perspective. I walk away. When I return, I usually know what needs to be withdrawn in order to move forward. I am as objective as possible and courageous enough to admit that whatever this element is, it is not adding value to the greater good. This does not mean that it is not inherently valuable; it simply is ineffective in the current context.

Subtraction leaves things to the imagination and puts it in an active state, which is much more seductive and compelling than spelling it all out. There are times when I include images of people in my work, and I always remove or obscure faces because I want the viewers to see themselves or someone they know, not a particular given identity.

In this way they can emotionally connect to and personally participate in the work, which is the artist's ultimate objective.

Sometimes you won't know what to subtract until you have added. This process applies to all endeavors, not just creative ones. It is also, I find, a way of maneuvering through life.

Lisa Occhipinti (locchipinti.com) is an artist and the author of The Repurposed Library, *featured in the* New York Times. *Her piece "Perfect Balance" appears on the next page.*

ONE LESS IF

Markus Flanagan

Because we are in the business of make-believe, actors are highly prone to catastrophize. It's not outrageous to think that you can be unknown today and a household name six months later. In an effort to exercise what small amount of control we have over our careers, actors fantasize the ups and downs of work and life with too many ifs:

"*If* I get this audition, and *if* I nail it and get the job, and *if* the director and the producers like what I do enough, I could become a series regular, and *if* the show runs ten seasons I'll be a multimillionaire."

And the reverse:

"*If* I don't nail the audition, and *if* the casting director doesn't like me, and *if* she tells the other casting directors in town how bad I did, I'm not getting called back and my agent will drop me, and *if* my agent drops me, I'm damaged goods and no one will sign me again. So *if* I don't nail this audition, my career is over."

We'll do that even before we've read the audition material. We see the whole fantastic picture. Now, we are taught to see the dream, to visualize our success, right? We're told we can mentally *will* our success to come true. Not totally bad advice, but this isn't about dreaming; this is about keeping your psyche clear so your artistry can flourish. Ifs create expectations based in fear. Fear won't make your acting better and can make it worse.

Actors get jobs by acting. I counsel actors to consider just the ifs that will lead to a better audition. Subtract as many ifs as it takes for you to get back to what you can truly influence and leave out the rest. That will settle your brain and prepare you to act:

"IF I go in and give myself over to the role, I'll leave feeling like all the time and effort I've spent getting there has been well spent and I'll have given myself a good shot at getting a job. IF they are looking for someone like me, I will have given them their best option, and I'll leave knowing I did the best I could to better my career today. IF I don't execute, I have to ask myself what stopped me."

By subtracting ifs, you add the proper perspective and give yourself a shot at doing good work. Good work will become a job. That's the most you should put on any one event. You act and you leave.

So IF you want to keep your sanity, subtract the ifs that had you either getting a star on Hollywood Boulevard or never working in this town again.

Markus Flanagan (onelessbitteractor.com) is a veteran actor, a coach, and the author of One Less Bitter Actor, *with a vision that only art can save the world.*

SAY NO MORE

Carmine Gallo

As a communications coach, I've learned that subtraction can mean the difference between a highly persuasive presentation and a long, convoluted, and confusing one. In my own experience I've noticed that speakers who deliver presentations with fewer words carry themselves better. They have leadership presence. They've internalized the story and are confident about their message. People who fill their slides with words and bullet points are often unsure of the material and speak with less passion and conviction.

The power of subtraction hit me when I watched Steve Jobs introduce the first MacBook Air in 2008. Most speakers would have created a slide filled with bullet points. All Jobs said was, "Today we're introducing a computer that is so thin, it fits inside one of those interoffice envelopes you see floating around the workplace." The slide he showed had no words, just a photo showing a hand pulling a MacBook Air out of a manila envelope. No words; the image said it all.

Why say more when you can say less?

I remember helping a large technology company with its annual investors meeting. I tried to persuade them to subtract words to make their presentations more effective. The room was filled with engineering types who would rather shrink the font to seven points than eliminate a word.

Finally, the company CEO stood up and told everyone to give it a try. The first slide had one simple sentence that summed up the company's vision in just eight words. At the end of the presentation a consensus of analysts said it was the best investor update in the company's 20-year history. When asked what they would remember most, several analysts quoted the first slide word for word. Subtraction actually made the remaining words on the screen more memorable.

Always ask yourself, How can I reduce the clutter? Steve Jobs once said the secret of innovation is to "say no to a thousand things." I believe the same philosophy applies to the art of communication. By saying "no" more often, you'll be more successful in getting your prospects to say "yes."

Carmine Gallo (carminegallo.com) is the founder of Gallo Communications and the author of The Presentation Secrets of Steve Jobs *and* The Apple Experience.

STAND OUT OR DON'T BOTHER

Sally Hogshead

Every day, you're in a battle for attention. Every day, you do battle against a thousand shiny objects to keep someone's attention. Smartphones, tablets, laptops—powerful diversions full of noise with the potential to sabotage the very signal you're sending.

If you can't stand out, you can't win. If you can't stand out, don't even bother playing. There are too many options, too many competitors willing to take your place. Today your success will depend on your ability to subtract the diversions.

In the battle for attention, you have a secret weapon: *fascination*.

Fascination is an intense emotional focus. When you fascinate people, they become completely focused on you. They stop focusing on all the shiny objects competing for their attention and focus completely on your message. The noise disappears, and they hear only your signal.

You can achieve this kind of intense emotional focus by understanding your natural ability to fascinate others. I can say this for a fact: *you* are fascinating.

But for you to eliminate diversions from the equation and create this intense focus, you must identify and apply your natural fascination. We each have a natural talent for attracting attention. It's natural, so you don't have to fake it or rehearse it—it's already there, hardwired into your personality. You just have to identify it and use it.

Once you understand that unique strength, you can exploit it. Your listeners become more alert and focused, and your message is their priority. You become far more persuasive in communicating anything—selling life insurance to 20-year-olds becomes possible; inspiring a people during a round of layoffs becomes possible; convincing the gate agent to give you the last seat on the last flight out becomes possible.

Your goal is not to dazzle people with a variety of messages. No. Quite the opposite. Your goal is to pare down and attract their focus to just one thing: you.

So figure out what makes you fascinating, what makes you "you." The world doesn't need more messages. It needs more of you and less of the rest. It needs your secret best practices, your offbeat observations, your old-fashioned advice, and your cutting-edge solutions.

It's not enough to communicate—you must also captivate. You must *be* the shiny object.

So subtract the noise and add the signal. Stand out or don't bother.

Sally Hogshead (sallyhogshead.com) is the bestselling author of Fascinate: Your 7 Triggers for Persuasion and Captivation.

PULL, DON'T PUSH

Shawn Parr

One of my favorite stories concerns the opening of a 30,000-square-foot Virgin store in a small British town the likes of which had never been seen in that community. The interior was beautiful and housed countless cool brands. On the day the store opened to the public, great bands played in the entrance, local celebrities were on hand, and the well-supported hometown football team was there in all its glory. The big publicity push was in full swing.

Opening day was a huge success and got significant press coverage. But the star attraction wasn't the store or the celebrities; it was an old stone owl.

This little guy had stood on the top of the building for over a century and a half. Less than a foot tall, he'd scared countless flocks of pigeons away and in the process fulfilled his job of stopping them from tainting the Victorian facade of the building.

During the recent renovation, a workman had asked Virgin if they wanted to keep the owl. Of course they did. After all, the old bird had seen many store owners come and go during his unrelenting watch. Someone got the idea to build him a cool perch, suspending him over the store's main stairway, giving him his own slightly tongue-in-cheek commemoration plaque as a small but unique local historical character.

All in all, to clean, mount, install, and brand the little owl, it cost about thirty pounds, versus the million or so invested in the store itself.

Not only did that thirty pounds give them some great local publicity coverage, it gave them an ongoing talking point. Despite the store being part of a large nationwide chain, the brand was recognized as being respectful of the city's local history and for having a warm personality and a wry but fun sense of humor.

That little bird achieved what all the advertising, marketing, branding, promotion, and publicity efforts couldn't: pulling people in.

When you look for genuine emotional connections to a community, create stories from the simplest things, look at the minutiae to differentiate yourself, and dare to be a bit silly. The littlest touches can pay the biggest dividends.

Shawn Parr (bulldogdrummond.com) is "the Guvner" of Bulldog Drummond, a design and innovation consultancy based in San Diego, California.

FIGHTING EXCESS

Justin Brady

I was lucky. My very first project and client taught me a lesson about subtraction.

It was a small coffee shop owned by an Ethiopian woman in New Brighton, Minnesota, just on the edge of Minneapolis. She had hired me to design a logo for her shop. In the course of research I kept seeing the same coffee pot, called a *jebena*, typically used in the Ethiopian coffee ceremony. It was beautiful, and it became the visual anchor to celebrate this Ethiopian coffee shop.

I kept drawing the *jebena* over and over again. Somehow I wanted to combine the coffee bean and the *jebena* in the logo but didn't want two visuals to compete or conflict with each other for space and attention. I kept drawing and drawing, not satisfied. Finally I just sort of stumbled on the idea of using the shape of the bean in negative space for the handle opening of the *jebena*. Now that's probably an eye roller for most designers, but for me, just starting out, it was a little eureka moment.

The ability to edit is critical for a designer. If there's anything visually present that doesn't assist in sending the message directly or emotionally, it's a distraction and will work against the design. Achieving simplicity by removing distraction is always the goal, but it's a discipline, and if I'm not diligent, I can succumb to excess.

Recently, I was working on a project for a family farm in Iowa. On all their packaging we thought it would be visually appealing to have their logo appear as though it were stamped on.

I started thinking about how cool it would be if each stamp was printed to look hand stamped. I'd need about ten different effects, I figured, to do a custom package printing. It was sophisticated and expensive. In fact, it was prohibitive for the family farm.

I was desperate to salvage the project. I went back through my notes, and when I did, the most elegant solution of them all hit me like a slap to the forehead: an actual stamp! The farm already had to handle all the meat individually before giving it to customers, so hand stamping each package would be a breeze.

I passed this solution on to them, and they loved the idea. They loved that it didn't cost tens of thousands of dollars—more like fifty bucks—and that it was so simple.

In design, as in most things, fighting excess is a constant battle.

Justin Brady (testoftimedesign.com) is the founder of Test of Time Design, a design consultancy based in Des Moines, Iowa.

ATTENTION DEFICIT

Mary Poppendieck

When Mark Parker became CEO of Nike, Steve Jobs called to congratulate him. Parker asked Jobs if he had any advice, and at first the answer was no, but then Jobs said, "Well, I do have some advice. Nike makes some of the best products in the world—products that you lust after, absolutely beautiful, stunning products. But you also make a lot of crap. Just get rid of the crappy stuff and focus on the good stuff." Parker later said, "I expected a little laugh, but there was a pause and no laugh at the end."

I had the same experience when I wrote my first book. It took me about six months to write the first draft. I submitted it to the editor, who sent it out to reviewers, and in a few weeks I had a rather unanimous verdict: there was some good stuff but a lot of crap. It was a random collection of articles, not a book. When I reread the book from the distance of a few months, I had to agree. It lacked a theme, a structure, and flow.

I reorganized the material and threw out more than half of what I had written. I had a new set of criteria: I imagined that two managers I had worked with recently were reading every paragraph. I focused on whether they were getting bored. Now these managers were rather impatient, so I figured they were easily bored. And if I thought they were getting bored, the paragraph was discarded. I didn't need it. I needed a more concise and effective way to get my point across. Or maybe the point was not that important in the first place.

I had three simple rules for that book: first, my readers would not, could not get bored; second, the content had to flow seamlessly from one section to the next, without expecting my reader to jump around; and third, there would be no duplication. I pretended that I was the reader and demanded that I didn't waste my time with extra words, extra ideas, scattered content, or duplication.

My lesson in all of this: attention is a scarce commodity. Make sure you don't squander it. Spend time deciding what you will not do so that you can focus on the good stuff.

Mary Poppendieck (poppendieck.com) with her husband, Tom, is a cofounder of Poppendieck.LLC and the coauthor most recently of Leading Lean Software Development.

LAW NO. 4

CREATIVITY THRIVES

UNDER INTELLIGENT

CONSTRAINTS

Art consists of limitation.
The most beautiful part of every picture is the frame.
G. K. Chesterton

Astrid Klein and Mark Dytham did not set out to launch a global wave of creativity. They were simply trying to figure out how to make a go of Super Deluxe, a tiny basement venue they owned in Tokyo that wasn't doing very well. The two architects, name partners in the Tokyo-based firm Klein Dyson architecture (KDa), weren't having much luck renting out the underground gallery/club/bar/lounge/performance space/creative kitchen. On a lark they decided to invite some architect colleagues over to spend an evening sharing their work and engaging in a bit of *pecha kucha* (peh-CHAHK-chah), a Japanese phrase meaning "chitchat."

There was a catch, or rather several catches. First, it was a formal sharing by way of a stand-up presentation. Second, each presenter had only 6 minutes and 40 seconds to show his or her work. As Mark and Astrid tell it, the rationale behind the time limit was simple: "Because architects talk too much! Give a microphone and some images to an architect—or most creative people for that matter—and they'll go on forever! Give PowerPoint to anyone else and they have the same problem."

There were three other constraints: if you wanted to participate, you had to show exactly 20 images, each one for exactly 20 seconds, and those images were advanced automatically by a timer while you spoke. But the time constraint wasn't as arbitrary as it sounds. Mark told NPR in a 2010 interview that he and Astrid "were trying to find a catchy five minutes or so for the architect to present." What they settled on was a Goldilocks formula: 10 slides at 10 seconds per slide was too short, and 30 slides at 30 seconds per slide was too long; 20 by 20 was just right and made for an effective, efficient, entertaining, and rather elegant presentation. It further enabled the duo to squeeze 20 speechlets into a single evening.

The first night went so well that the two planned another for the next month, dubbing it PechaKucha Night. PechaKucha Night soon became a popular monthly event, with the audience growing in size to hundreds and participants other than architects wanting in. Drinking, thinking, and networking proved to be an irresistible draw for the creative set, including designers, artists, and scholars. It wasn't long before the problem of what to do with Super Deluxe was no longer an issue.

Word began to spread beyond Tokyo, and after three years and 30 events, PechaKucha Nights began cropping up in other cities. Astrid and Mark put up pecha-kucha.org to announce new venues and events, and within another two years PechaKucha Night had gained an international presence. By 2010, PechaKucha Night had gone viral to over 230 cities all across the world, with new cities coming on board every few days.

When you go to a PechaKucha Night—I've been to several and participated in two—you're struck by the creative energy flowing through the people and the place. The description on pecha-kucha.org is accurate:

> PechaKucha Nights are informal and fun gatherings where creative people get together and share their ideas, works, thoughts, holiday snaps—just about anything really, in the PechaKucha 20x20 format. PechaKucha Nights are mostly held in fun spaces with a bar. Anyone can present—this is the beauty of PechaKucha Nights. It has turned into a massive celebration, with events happening in hundreds of cities around the world, inspiring creatives worldwide.

I first heard the term in 2005 from a colleague at Toyota who had just returned from a visit to the company headquarters in Japan. When he described it to me, I didn't get it. I couldn't imagine the attraction. It wasn't until I read a short article two years later on the *Wired* website, penned by Daniel Pink and accompanied by a video of his own *pecha kucha*, that I began to see the challenge and potential of it. I've since used it on many occasions and teach it as a technique for pitching creative ideas.

Pecha kucha shares the constraint of time with the very popular TED talks. TED is a nonprofit organization founded in 1984 that brings together people from the three worlds of technology, entertainment, and design to share "Ideas Worth Spreading." Through two major conferences and hundreds of minor ones, a paying audience can hear the most creative people on the planet talk about their work in 18-minute (or less) presentations. Although speaking at a TED event is by invitation only and an invitation is considered an honor, TED at its core is a kindred spirit to *pecha kucha*: both began as a small gathering to share stimulating ideas within a time limit to keep things moving and lively.

What both formats have in common is the fourth law of subtraction: *Creativity thrives under intelligent constraints.*

The magic of the constraint—whether it's an 18-minute TED talk or a 6-minute and 40-second *pecha kucha*—lies in the ability of a boundary or limit to provide both a focus and a framework, which is exactly what the human brain needs to make the neural pathways that connect the dots into the kind of thought that we call creativity. Also, both TED and PechaKucha Night are unconventional, unorthodox frameworks: they send the signal that something is different and thus that we need to think differently.

As TED host Chris Anderson explains the 18-minute constraint: "By forcing speakers who are used to going on for 45 minutes to bring it down to 18, you get them to really think about what they want to say. What is the key point they want to communicate? It has a clarifying effect. It brings discipline." It's like a child's sandbox: more creative play will occur inside the sandbox than in the entire backyard.

I spoke at a London TED event in November 2010. Compared to *pecha kucha*, a TED talk is a walk in the park. The constraints are not nearly as daunting as those of *pecha kucha*. Interestingly, though, the theme of the event was "Reframe." Although this chapter began with a popular quote by the British writer G. K. Chesterton, I began my talk with a quote from Frank Zappa: "The most important thing in art is the frame. For paint, literally, for other arts, figuratively—because, without this humble appliance, you can't know where the art stops and the real world begins."

Zappa and Chesterton have it right in elevating the figurative frame to the level of art itself, as it is the constraints—the canvas edge, the marble block, the musical octave, the structural limits of language—that spark and spur creativity while bringing the art of subtraction front and center. Michelangelo's statue of David would not be considered the masterpiece it is had he chosen to mold it from clay rather than sculpt it from marble, a subtractive endeavor involving an unyielding and unforgiving material.

Framing is every bit as important when it comes to creatively solving complex problems in areas other than pure art. The ability to properly frame an issue or problem goes far in avoiding the typical pitfalls that limit our ability to reach a creative solution. Setting intelligent constraints will not only reveal the most creative thinkers in the room, it will also work to attract them to the challenge in the first place. The experience can be as exhilarating for the creator as the outcome is memorable for those looking on.

It is as important to see how that works as it is to understand why it works.

MISSION: IMPOSSIBLE

It's one thing to give a time-constrained talk for a few minutes; it's quite another to send a spaceship into space on a shoestring. It takes a special kind of person to be inspired by a mandate riddled with risk and having little margin for error, such as the one issued by NASA to its Jet Propulsion Laboratory (JPL) in Pasadena, California: "Take risks but don't fail."

Such a person is Brian Muirhead, who at age 41 in 1993 accepted the job as flight systems manager of the Mars Pathfinder project and with it the NASA challenge to land a cutting-edge, remote-controlled robotic all-terrain rover on Mars that would reliably beam back images, collect samples, and return scientific data on the red planet. The only catch: he was given just three years and $150 million to do it. The immediately preceding Mars Observer, which carried a $1 billion price tag and had taken 10 years, had just been lost in space, an embarrassing failure for the U.S. space program. No one in his or her right mind would want to manage the next Mars project, if indeed there was one. At the time Brian accepted the job, project funding was not guaranteed.

Brian is a quiet, cerebral, and unassuming rocket scientist. Now chief engineer at JPL, he has a significantly bigger title, significantly less hair, and significantly more white in his beard than when I first met him, undoubtedly as a result of his almost 35 years of intense involvement with high-profile missions in pursuit of JPL's mission to push the outer edge of space exploration.

Brian was a frequent visitor to the Toyota campus during my tenure there. After reading his 1999 book *High Velocity Leadership*, we invited Brian to guest speak about the Mars Pathfinder project, and he soon became a regular fixture in the University of Toyota's "lean" leadership curriculum. Through the sessions I became quite familiar with Brian and his saga. It was and remains one of the most compelling examples of how to use seemingly impossible constraints to tap into and guide human creativity in a team setting.

"Faster, better, cheaper" was the phrase used by a frustrated Mark Albrecht, staff director for the White House National Space Council, in a 1990 article he published calling for new management approaches at NASA. Albrecht's plea responded to a series of multi-billion-dollar NASA proposals for returning to the moon and exploring human expeditions to Mars: "the basic goal is to do things faster, cheaper, safer, better." The wholesale failure of the 1992 Mars Observer project sealed NASA's fate, and in early 1992 President George Bush appointed a new NASA administrator, Dan Goldin. Goldin laid out the "faster, better, cheaper" approach in a speech he gave later that year:

> We should send a series of small and medium-sized robotic spacecraft to all the planets and major moons, as well as some asteroids and comets. Let's see how many we can build that weigh hundreds, not thousands, of pounds; that use cutting-edge technology, not 10-year-old technology that plays it safe; that cost tens of millions, not billions; and take months and years, not decades, to build and arrive at their destination. Slice through the Gordian knot of big, expensive spacecraft that take forever to finish. By building them assembly line style, we can launch lots of them, so if we lose a few due to the riskier nature of high technology, it won't be the scientific disaster or blow to national prestige that it is when you pile everything on one probe and launch it every ten years.

In 1993, Goldin announced that JPL would explore a return to the surface of Mars by looking for creative ways to achieve the objectives of the failed Mars Observer project with a series of smaller missions. Mars Pathfinder was the first of those missions. Goldin's accepting attitude toward failure was fine in theory, but in reality his attitude was quite different: "Pathfinder could not and must not fail," Brian told us. "But judging by the looks on the faces of the thirty or so people staring at me when I walked into that first project meeting at JPL, the mission was impossible."

"The constraints were impossible," Brian would say. "Unheard of. Crazy. We were being asked to do a major NASA mission for less than what it cost to produce the movie *Titanic*. And provide a happy ending to boot! The Viking mission to Mars in the late 1970s took seven years to develop, and we had three. But for whatever reason, maybe because it was that risky, it had a magnetic attraction for me."

Impossible is a word that you never quite get accustomed to, although it does get less surprising. I heard it repeatedly at Toyota, as did everyone.* It rang through the halls of Toyota when in 1987 the chief engineer for the secret project that would become the first Lexus, Ichiro Suzuki, issued the challenge of producing a luxury performance sedan that would beat the best luxury sedans—BMW 735i and Mercedes 420SEL—across the board in comfort, styling, performance, handling, cabin noise, aerodynamics, weight, and fuel efficiency. His goals included a top speed of 155 miles per hour (735i and 420SEL topped out at under 140), 22.5 miles per gallon (735i and 420SEL got less than 20), a cabin noise level of 58 decibels at 60 mph (735i and 420SEL were over 60), and an aerodynamic drag of 0.29 or less (735i and 420SEL were over 0.32), all in a vehicle weighing 80 pounds less than the 3,880-pound 735i.

The reaction from the 1,400 engineers involved was unanimous: *impossible*. Legend has it that the product engineering chief, Akira Takahashi, told Suzuki to his face that he was out of his mind, refusing to go along with the plan. The goals were too high individually, but together? Impossible. Takahashi's argument made sense: no Toyota car could go faster than 110 mph except the Supra, which at its top end of 130 nearly became airborne. Suzuki planted himself in Takahashi's office, refusing to leave until Takahashi agreed to try. To this day, Suzuki, now retired, will smile and repeat: *impossible*.

---

* My pet theory on how constraints in the form of selective scarcity became such an integral part of the Toyota organizational genetics is a simple one: necessity. World War II devastated industrial Japan, and Toyota Motor Corporation was not spared. The need to survive and thrive amid a scarcity of business essentials—land, facilities, finances, and skilled labor—required a new way of thinking and conducting business. Intent on competing successfully in the world automotive market but lacking the luxury of ample resources, Toyota did the only thing it could do: leverage the one resource it did have—human creativity.

Dramatic Destination

Impossible. Unheard of. Crazy. Those are the words of breakthrough. Those are fighting words to the right person. The right people will hold on to the creative tension between clearly conflicting objectives. They will leverage the scarcity of resources. They will reframe constraints to be the very source of innovation. And they will find a way to get the job done without compromising the dramatic destination.

"That's the secret," as Brian Muirhead says. "You have to point your team, your people, toward a dramatic destination." Landing on the surface of Mars in three years for $150 million is dramatic. Beating the best luxury performance sedans on the planet when you've never built one before—essentially building the best car in the world—is a dramatic destination. Every time Brian would retell his story, we'd look at each other, smile, and nod: "Lexus."

Dramatic destinations are all well and good and get the blood boiling. But what Brian emphasized and what Ichiro Suzuki knew was that dramatic destinations must be broken down into tactical targets: working-level goals that people can own and focus on. In other words, to grow a forest, you have to tend to each individual tree without losing sight of the forest. "That's where leadership comes in," Brian says. "A creative leader is both the glue and the grease. Keep the moving parts moving, together, and in the same direction."

Dramatic destinations demand different thinking. Those facing the Pathfinder and Lexus teams called for bold and radically creative solutions. Designing a vehicle, though—whether a car, plane, or spaceship—is often an act of sacrifice and compromise. But Ichiro Suzuki's war cry was *naukatsu*, which means "never compromise." And as Brian Muirhead would say, "it was crystal clear that we would simply have to throw the rule book away."

The issues facing Lexus engineers were many, conflicting, and complex. Greater speed and acceleration conflicts directly with fuel efficiency, noise, and weight, because higher speed and acceleration requires a more powerful engine. A more powerful engine is a bigger and heavier engine, and so it makes more noise and consumes more fuel. A smooth, quiet ride conflicts directly with lower weight and better handling at high speed. Heavy, non-performance-oriented cars with beefier insulation and a softer suspension provide the smoother, quieter ride. Refined styling and high-speed stability conflict directly with aerodynamic drag; the more angled look of 1980s luxury cars provided greater stability because of the higher air friction. Suzuki demanded a V8 engine with a 4-liter displacement, something unheard of in a lightweight, fuel-efficient, quiet luxury car.

For Brian Muirhead, it wasn't so much the launch as the landing that posed an enormous challenge. There are two ways to land on the surface of another planet. The first way is called a propulsive descent. It's the traditional approach used by Apollo missions to land on the moon and by previous Mars missions, such as the Viking mission of 1976: you use a big rocket burn on approach to enter orbit and slow down and then use another big rocket burn to escape orbit and land on the surface. This way is tried and true, safe and sensible. The only problem is that that option required a much bigger launch vehicle, a lot of additional hardware, and far too much money for the budget constraint.

The only option was to head directly into Mars at an interplanetary speed of about 16,500 miles per hour. Few missions—by anyone, anywhere—had attempted the direct approach, and none had been attempted with Mars. "This was the first time anyone had even attempted to enter Mars's atmosphere directly," said Brian. "We had to really thread the needle to survive entry." A direct landing required entering the Martian atmosphere at just the right angle, with little margin for error. But budget constraints left no other alternative. The question was: how do you slow down enough to land safely?

What both Brian Muirhead and Ichiro Suzuki realized early on was that thinking differently often requires fresh eyes, open minds, and youthful energy.

A Tale of Two 25s

Nicknamed Dezi, Akihiro Nagaya was all of 25 years old when Ichiro Suzuki handpicked him to join the nine other designers working on the Lexus prototype design team. Dezi had no experience; in fact, he was still in design school when he went to work for Toyota in 1983. Suzuki liked his ambition and drive and kept an eye on the youngster, who in the four years before joining the Lexus team had demonstrated raw talent and a flair for bold ideas. Suzuki knew Dezi would bring that energy with him and breathe new life into the design team, all of whose members except Dezi were seasoned vets.

Dezi had a unique perspective on automobiles. As a youth in Japan, he had fallen in love with automobiles the moment he drove one. But for him, a car wasn't just a car. Cars were, in his words, "moving sculpture," and he wanted to be the one to sculpt them. It was exactly the kind of thinking Suzuki was looking for in tackling the impossible constraints, since sculpture is by definition a subtractive art. It was exactly the perspective that would save the Lexus design from falling well short of something worthy of the world's best car.

Projects in pursuit of dramatic destinations demand flexibility in execution and the ability to recognize when to tack. It's like sailing, in which you're at the mercy of changing winds and know you can't go on a straight line to get where you want to go, especially if you can't see the destination. You have to zigzag your way to get there, all the time keeping your eye on the horizon and the North Star for guidance. Efficient tacking is the key to your success. But what do you do when the wind dies?

Late in the game, the Lexus project stalled, and the project team got stuck on two key challenges. The first was fuel efficiency, which gave the team the most difficulty. There was a very serious practical consideration, which was avoiding the gas guzzler tax of $1,000 per car not rated at 22.5 miles per gallon or better. There was also a point of pride: to that point, no luxury car had avoided it, and Suzuki wanted Lexus to be the first to do so.

One of the most effective ways to boost a car's fuel efficiency is to reduce its coefficient of drag, or aerodynamic friction. A good way to do that is to emulate the shape of a teardrop: you raise the rear deck and sculpt the exterior shape. A lower front end helps, as does streamlining the underbody. The problem was that in the late 1980s, luxury styling was all about lines and angles, and cars like that aren't very aerodynamic. Shackled by that mental model, the designers and engineers simply hit an impasse after dozens of attempts and failed wind tunnel tests.

The second challenge concerned the front-end design: nothing about it satisfied Suzuki. Stubborn and subscribing to the notion that harmony consists of opposing tensions like that of a bow or a lyre, he believed that styling, comfort, and performance could, and in this case *must*, coexist harmoniously in a car such that it would be as calming as warm bath yet invigorating at the same time, more "like a warm bath after an hour of yoga."

To that point, Dezi had been quiet, working on lesser design challenges. Out of ideas, the senior designer, Kunihiro Uchida, asked Dezi to take a crack at sketching what he thought the front end should look like. "I was asked to create a front that would save the ass of the [Lexus] LS," Dezi would recall later.

And save he did. "Flow. I focused on flow," Dezi said. To him, the transitions between the various elements suggested that each of these seemingly contradictory notions had to be seamless. The only alternative was to refine luxury styling. Dezi described it this way: "You have to actualize impossible combinations." The sketch depicted flowing lines with smooth transitions, without lines and angles. As he tells it, when he saw the sketch, Suzuki shouted, "This is it!" "It was quite a risky gamble to count on a rookie for such a critical sketch," Dezi said. "I have special respect for Suzuki's decision and Kunihiro's management to let me do it."

Dezi's design helped get the team unstuck and opened the floodgates of creativity to allow solutions to begin to emerge. What had been seen as contradictions began to be reframed and seen as complementary. Aesthetics and aerodynamics could complement each other, for example, by fitting window glass and door handles into the metal itself, producing a cleaner look and better airflow. Sloping the rear window just enough to push air off the trunk and building a spoiler into the trunk lid to make the back end more stable enabled a sleeker profile. The innovations kept coming.

In a reversal of conventional design wisdom, function began to follow form, and mechanical components were redesigned in dramatic fashion. The engine was cast almost entirely from aluminum—block, pistons, valve lifters, cam covers, everything—saving 120 pounds. The propeller shaft, originally in two parts connected by an angled knuckle—like most rear-wheel-drive cars at the time—was replaced by a perfectly straight one, enabling a nearly silent cabin.

Tommasso "Tom" Rivellini was also just 25 when he came to the Mars Pathfinder team as a hardware systems designer. He had never even held a design job, much less designed hardware for a mission. But to solve the design challenge of landing safely on the surface of Mars, Brian Muirhead was looking for someone and something you can't find on paper. He didn't follow the traditional human resources approach of matching résumé credentials with job requirements.

"We hired some of our best people without any of the conventional evidence that they could do the job," Brian would say. "We had energy, we had drive, we had enthusiasm, but not necessarily a lot of experience. So that's what we were looking for, and that's what we liked about Tom. He had that drive, that ingenuity. Nobody had done what we were trying to do before, so Tom looked to be as talented as anybody. Very creative. But more than anything, Tom had the drive."

Little did Tom know that Brian's boss, project manager Tony Spear, would soon become fond of throwing his arm around Tom and saying, "Hey, everybody, the whole mission is riding on this guy right here."

Here's Tom on taking the job: "You know, basically I was too ignorant to know that I was getting in way over my head, and I actually think most people were too ignorant just in terms of what the Pathfinder spacecraft development was going to turn into to know that they should never have given me this job. But nonetheless, I got the job, and I just, you know, I woke every morning and was just totally enthusiastic about it and just totally loved it. And so it was easy to put in many hours and weekends and everything that it took to make it happen."

The "it" Tom is referring to is the radically creative approach to landing the Pathfinder on Mars: air bags. Pathfinder would

Image courtesy of AstroBio.

121

head straight into the Martian atmosphere, slowing its descent first by para-chute and then by air bags just before the craft hit the ground. "It was a wild idea," Brian would say. "Use giant air bags to cushion the lander's im-pact, then let it bounce and roll to a stop? NASA basically just looked at it and said, 'Well, propulsion; that's the old way of doing business. You guys will never get this job done if you do it the old way; it's too expensive, so, try it.'"

Try was the operative word. As Tom would later tell the story in NASA's online magazine *Astrobiology*:

> Our task was to design and build airbags for Pathfinder's landing on Mars, an approach that had never been used on any mission. Airbags may seem like a simple, low-tech product, but it was eye-opening to discover just how little we knew about them. We knew that the only way to find out what we needed to learn was to build prototypes and test them. We just didn't know how ignorant we were going to be.
>
> Airbags seemed like a crazy idea to a lot of people. Nobody ever said that, mind you, but there seemed to be a widespread feeling that the airbags weren't going to work. "We'll let you guys go off and fool around until you fall flat on your faces." That was the unspoken mes-sage I received day after day.
>
> Everyone's main fear about using these giant airbags was that the lander would be buried in an ocean of fabric when the airbags deflated. I began the search for a solution by building scale models of the airbags and lander, and I played with them in my office for a couple of months.
>
> I built the models out of cardboard and plastic, and taped them up with packing tape I got from the hardware store and ribbon from the fabric store. I used a small raft inflator that I had at home to pump up my model airbags. Over and over again, I filled the miniature air-bags and then let them deflate, watching what happened.
>
> I fooled around with a dozen or more approaches before I finally came up with something that I thought worked. Slowly but surely, I came up with the idea of using cords that zigzag through belt loops inside the airbags. Pull the cords a certain way, and the cords would

draw in all of the fabric and contain it. Wait to open the lander until after all of the airbags had retracted, and the fabric would be tucked neatly underneath.

Testing, Testing: Check 1, Check 2

A creative design does not become a viable innovation until it actually works. The Lexus and Pathfinder teams obsessed over testing. That's understandable in light of the fact that human lives in the case of Lexus and millions of dollars in the case of Pathfinder were at stake. Both projects involved a lot of trial and error, as both projects involved things that had never been done before.

"My boss, Tony Spear, had one mantra from the very beginning," Brian would tell us. "Test, test, test." Using air bags meant the Pathfinder would be bouncing when it landed. Tom Rivellini conducted dozens of tests using helicopters that dropped the air-bag-wrapped Pathfinder hundreds of feet onto a Mars-like surface, starting with a 1/20 scale model and working up to full scale. Each test produced important new refinements, but the first drops were complete failures. "We weren't sure if this thing was going to work," Brian would say. "But we kept working the details, improving the design, and going back in to test. It was a very iterative process."

I'll never forget the story of how the team tried the analytical approach but ended up burning over a week of Cray supercomputer time to get just a few seconds of fairly worthless data on the impact. "The problem was just too complex," Brian said. "So we had to rely on Tom and his team's ability to design, build, and test their way to a design that would work."

Here's how Tom told the story of testing in his *Astrobiology* post:

> Even after we had the mechanics figured out for the airbags, a big question remained: What about the rocky Martian terrain? Landing on Mars, we had to accept whatever Mother Nature gave us. The Pathfinder wouldn't have a landing strip. To simulate conditions on Mars, we brought in large lava rocks the size of a small office desk. They were real lava rocks that our geologists had gone out and picked; if you tried to handle one of them, you would cut up your hands.

The more landscape simulations we tested, the more we started tearing up the airbags. Things were not looking good. Once again, we realized that this was an area that we just didn't understand. We tried material after material, applying them in dozens of different configurations to the outside of the airbag. Each test became like a ritual, because it took between eight and ten hours to prepare the system including transporting the airbags into the vacuum chamber, getting all of the instrumentation wired up, raising the airbags up to the top of the chamber, making sure all the rocks were in the right place. The vacuum chamber where we did the drop tests used so much power that we were only able to test in the middle of the night. Once the doors of the vacuum chamber were closed, it took three or four hours just to pump down the chamber. At that point, everybody either broke for dinner or went to relax for a while, before coming back at midnight or whatever the appointed hour was. Then we had another 45 minutes of going over all of the instrumentation, going through checklists, and then ultimately the countdown.

The last 30 seconds of the countdown were excruciating. All of that anticipation, and then the whole impact lasted less than one second. When we finished a drop test, we knew right away whether it was a success or failure. Brian Muirhead, the flight systems manager, was always insistent that I call him immediately, no matter how late it was. At 4 a.m., I would call him at his home and have to give him the news, "Brian, we failed another test."

The day for the final test drop came, and Tom's plane from Los Angeles to the test site in Ohio was delayed. He told the team not to wait but to conduct the test without him and leave a videotape of the test for him to review. Tom recalls it this way:

When I got to the facility, the test crew wasn't there. I went into the control room and ran into the guy who processes the videotapes. "So what happened?" I asked him. "Did you guys do the test?" He pointed at a VCR and said, "The video is in there. Just go ahead and press play." So I hit play. Down comes the air bag in the video. It hits the platform and explodes catastrophically. My heart sank. We weren't going to make it. But then I realized that there was something strangely familiar about the video I had just watched. In an instant it came to me; they had put in the videotape from our worst drop test. The practical joke could mean only one thing: We had had a successful drop test and were finally good to go.

The entire Mars project from concept to touchdown was completed in 44 months—less than half the time needed for the 1970s Viking mission. The project team numbered just 300 members, a stark contrast to the 2,000 workers assigned to Viking. They also met their fixed budget, one-twentieth the cost of Viking.

On July 4, 1997, the Mars Pathfinder landed successfully on the red planet, and the tiny Sojourner rover started its now famous trek across the surface of Mars.

Mission: Accomplished.

The Lexus project took a total of six years from concept to launch: twice as long in development time as the Mars Pathfinder project. It would require the efforts of 1,400 designers and 3,700 engineers. Over 900 engine prototypes were developed and tested, along with 450 test models. Engineers spent hundreds of hours in wind tunnel tests and drove nearly 2 million test miles. Prototypes were dropped off and left in the Arizona desert for months with the windows down to observe the ravages of time and harsh exposure in an effort to create solutions to counteract those effects. The thickness of the chromium plating was increased dramatically, bodies were layered with six separate coats of paint, and a new laminated glass was created for the rear window to reduce sun damage.

When the Lexus LS400 made its debut on September 1, 1989, it stunned the automotive world and set a new luxury standard. It was by all objective measures the best car the world had ever seen. The facts made history: in every category rated by *Car and Driver*, the LS400 trumped the

BMW 735i and Mercedes 420SEL. The Lexus LS400 was five decibels quieter, 120 pounds lighter, and 17 miles per hour faster; got more than four more miles to the gallon; and retailed for $30,000 less than the BMW 735i. It then took just two years for Lexus to displace Mercedes-Benz and BMW, which had been entrenched for generations, as the top-selling luxury import nameplate in America.

Upon tearing down two LS400s given to General Motors headquarters by a southern California auto dealer, Cadillac engineers in Detroit concluded that the Lexus car could not possibly be built.

Mission: Accomplished.

CONSTRAINTS

Dan Roam uses the back of a napkin to scribble solutions to tough problems. Jessica Hagy of ThisIsIndexed.com offers brilliantly funny insights on 3 by 5 index cards. Hugh MacLeod of GapingVoid.com draws cartoons on the back of a business card. When I was working with Toyota, I learned how to use A3-size paper to propose solutions and strategies. When I worked with frog design, I learned to pitch ideas using a 6 by 9 idea sheet like the one shown here. Use the constraint of space to let your creative ideas shine.

ideasheet

dub it
a catchy and memorable name

describe it
briefly explain what it is

defend it
why it's important/valuable

draw it
sketch a preliminary prototype

THE CHAINS OF CREATIVITY

Why do constraints exert such a powerful influence on creativity? The idea that boundaries and limits can produce boundless and limitless thinking is counterintuitive and paradoxical. If we can understand a bit more about the mechanism behind constraints, perhaps sparking our creativity will become that much easier.

Yahoo! CEO Marissa Ann Mayer believes in the power of constraints, and offers an eloquent and thoughtful explanation of how they influence creativity. Before being named Yahoo's CEO in 2012, Marissa was Google's "gatekeeper," responsible for keeping the Google interface clean, simple, and uncluttered. Several years ago she revealed in an online post the philosophy of constraints that guides her work. "Creativity is often misunderstood," she begins. "People often think of it in terms of artistic work—unbridled, unguided effort that leads to beautiful effect. If you look deeper, however, you'll find that some of the most inspiring art forms— haikus, sonatas, religious paintings—are fraught with constraints."

Michelangelo would agree, with painting the Sistine Chapel being a case in point. Pope Julius II dreamed of a grand mausoleum for himself and commissioned Michelangelo as his artist of choice. Given carte blanche and unlimited resources, Michelangelo proposed an ambitious concept of more than 40 marble statues. After the initial design was approved, he spent nearly a year in the hills of Italy cutting massive marble blocks. But the Pope's advisors viewed Michelangelo as a threat to their influence and persuaded Julius to end the project before it began. On the advice of counsel, Julius then challenged Michelangelo to paint the Sistine Chapel as a fresco. It was a diabolical scheme. The Pope's advisors knew that Michelangelo not only detested painting as a medium but had no experience whatsoever with fresco. If Michelangelo accepted the commission, his anticipated failure would position him as inferior to Raphael, an up-and-comer who was being hailed as a genius. The comparison would destroy Michelangelo. However, if he refused, his career would end that day.

Caught between Charybdis and Scylla, Michelangelo did the only thing he could: use the impossible position to drive his creativity. Refusing the help of expert fresco painters brought in to advise him, he chose to completely reinvent the fresco technique. He even expanded the job's scope, deciding to paint the walls as well. He built his own scaffolding, locked himself in the chapel, and for four years contorted himself, hanging upside down, painting the incredibly beautiful scenes.

"They're beautiful because creativity triumphed over the rules," according to Marissa. Here's how she completes her thought.

> Constraints shape and focus problems, and provide clear challenges to overcome as well as inspiration. Creativity loves constraints, but they must be balanced with a healthy disregard for the impossible. Disregarding the bounds of what we know or what we accept gives rise to ideas that are nonobvious, unconventional, or simply unexplored. The creativity realized in this balance between constraint and disregard for the impossible are fueled by passion and result in revolutionary change.
>
> It's often easier to direct your energy when you start with constrained challenges . . . or constrained possibilities. . . . These constraints fuel passion and imagination. They generate creativity. . . . Constraints can give you speed and momentum. In shaping the process used to design a product, constraints can actually speed up development. Speed also lets you fail faster.
>
> But constraints alone can stifle and kill creativity. They can lead to pessimism and despair. So while we need constraints in order to fuel passion and insight, we also need a sense of hopefulness that keeps us engaged and unwaveringly in search of the right idea. It is from the interaction between constraint and the disregard for the impossible that unexpected insights, cleverness, and imagination are born. . . . True creativity makes the impossible possible. It can revolutionize a product, a business, the economy, and the world around us.

What I find intriguing and insightful about Marissa's explanation is this: although many creative activities—from the arts to design to athletics—all *seem* to be free-form in nature, in reality they are anything but. Each has its own set of limits that governs the performance by providing two very important elements: *focus* and *frame.*

Take comedy improvisation, for example: it is the audience that sets the limits. It is the audience that throws suggestions to the performers, themes that are often unlikely and, in the funniest skits, contradictory. The actors stitch the themes together with no further planning, and that sets the stage, as it were, for what happens next. And what happens next—on stage and between the performers—is much like what happens in a shared space such as Exhibition Road: behavior emerges within the given context, following the simplest rule: accept what is given to you by those with whom you are interacting. In comic improv, every line you produce builds on the line that comes right before it, and you can never question that line. This is a daunting constraint, because you cannot plan, prepare, or in any way rehearse your own lines. Your only choice is to remain focused and attuned to everything that is happening on stage, ready to react with nary a moment's notice. This simple limit, though, makes for nearly infinite possibilities and actually frees the performer to invoke his or her imagination.

When you learn comedy improv, you practice the technique of "yes, and. . . ." Not coincidentally, that is what the most effective creative brainstormers use in problem-solving sessions. It's the idea of building on others' ideas; when any idea is proposed, participants react to it with their own idea, beginning with "Yes, and. . . ."

All these examples—PechaKucha Night, a TED talk, Mars Pathfinder, Lexus LS400, the Sistine Chapel, and improvisational performance—have in common one thing: immovable obstacles. Recent studies offer evidence that, contrary to popular belief, the main event of the imagination—creativity—does not require unrestrained freedom; rather, it relies on limits and obstacles.

Researchers at the University of Amsterdam's Department of Social Psychology sought to prove that obstacles can prompt people to open their minds, look at the "big picture," and make connections between things that are not obviously connected. This ability is called "global processing," and is the hallmark of creativity. Participants in the study played a computer maze game. One group, though, played a version of the game that had an impassable blocking obstacle in one of the routes through the maze, which significantly limited options and made it much harder to discover the escape route. Then they were given a standard creativity test containing what psychologists term remote associates puzzles. Three remotely associated words appeared on the screen—for example, *plate, shot,* and *broken*—and the subjects were asked to find a fourth word that connected them all. (The answer is *glass.*) Those who had played the harder maze game containing the obstacle solved 40 percent more of the remote associates puzzles. The constraint had forced them into a more creative mindset, and their imaginations benefitted from first struggling with the obstacle in the maze.

"Daily life is full of obstacles," write the researchers in the November 2011 edition of *The Journal of Personality and Social Psychology.* "A construction site blocking the usual road to work, a colleague's background chatter interfering with one's ability to concentrate, a newborn child hindering parents in completing their daily routines, or a lack of resources standing in the way of realizing an ambitious plan. How do people cognitively respond to such obstacles? How do the ways in which they perceive and process information from their environment change when an obstacle interferes with what they want to accomplish?"

They answer those questions by concluding that it is not until we are faced with a difficult challenge or hurdle that we free ourselves from the cognitive chains that may be unconsciously inhibiting new connections waiting to be made in the right brain. They write: "Obstacles will prompt people to step back, broaden their perception, open up mental categories, and improve at integrating seemingly unrelated concepts." In other words, relevant obstacles, limits, and constraints make us (to borrow a phrase) "think different."

Raychem founder Paul Cook once told William Taylor in a *Harvard Business Review* interview: "To be an innovative organization, you have to ask for innovation. You assemble a group of talented people who are eager to do new things and put them in an environment where innovation is expected. It's that simple, and that hard." Dan Wieden, founder of the highly creative advertising agency Wieden+Kennedy, the firm behind Nike's "Just Do It" tagline, echoes Cook's sentiment by telling one journalist: "It really is that simple. You need to hire the best folks and then get out of the way."

In other words, give the right people the right challenge and trust that the solutions will appear. The Mars Pathfinder and Lexus LS400 missions illustrate how exceptional people facing monumental obstacles can rise to the occasion. But what is interesting in both cases is that it was the impossible goals that attracted those people to the project in the first place. And although those individuals were exceptional, they are not exceptions to the rule—they *are* the rule.

The rule is this: creativity thrives under intelligent constraints.

SILHOUETTES

IN SUBTRACTION

TINA SEELIG

DEREK SIVERS

TERESA AMABILE

PETER SIMS

SETH BERKOWITZ

HAL MACOMBER

DAN SCHAWBEL

MOE ABDOU

PAUL AKERS

PLAY ON WORDS

Tina Seelig

In my course on creativity and innovation at Stanford University, I decided to use a game to demonstrate that changing the constraints has a significant effect on creativity and team dynamics. I brought eight Scrabble boards to class and let the students play. Once they settled in, every 10 minutes I changed the rules of the game. Some of the new rules removed constraints, and others increased them.

For example, to reduce constraints, I allowed players to pick nine letters instead of seven, use proper names, or use foreign words. To increase constraints, I required players to add only four-letter words, build each new word onto the prior word only, or add a word to the board within a certain time limit.

The results were wonderfully surprising.

Whenever I loosened the rules, there was an audible cheer, and when I tightened the rules, the students groaned. But the cheers were misleading. You would think that the players would score more points and be more creative when the rules were looser. However, that was not the case. The students were more creative—and earned more points—when there were tighter constraints.

For example, when the rules were loosened to include proper names, one student put down a jumble of letters and claimed it was the name of her future child. Although it was funny, all agreed that this was a sloppy response rather than a creative solution. When the constraints were increased, the students had to be more creative. In addition, the competition around the board broke down. Those playing the game had to work together to reach their individual goals, and they collectively earned more points.

In the end, the students all felt that the original Scrabble rules have the perfect constraints and that is why the game has thrived so long. But they also realized that adding and subtracting constraints drastically changed their experience. They walked away with a new appreciation for the sensitive levers they have at their disposal when they manage or are part of creative teams.

They realized that they should fully appreciate the goals they have in mind and put constraints in place to inspire others to reach them.

Tina Seelig is executive director for the Stanford Technology Ventures Programs (stvp.stanford.edu) and the author of inGenius: A Crash Course on Creativity, *from which she adapted this story.*

SOUL CHAIN

Derek Sivers

Let's say you're a musician.

I say to you, "Write me a piece of music. Anything at all. Go."

"Umm . . . anything?" you say. "What kind of mood are you looking for? What genre?"

There are too many possibilities. The blank page problem.

How do you begin with infinity?

Now imagine I say, "Write me a piece of music, using only a xylophone, a flute, and a shoe box. You can only use four notes: B, C, E, F, and only two notes at a time. It has to be in 3/4 time, start quiet, get loud, then get quiet by the end. Make it sound like a ladybug dancing with an acorn. Go."

Ah . . . your imagination has already begun writing the music as soon as it hears the limitations. This is easy!

Those of us in developed countries—on fast Internet connections, reading books on subtraction just for fun—have a blank page. We can do anything. Anything we want. No restrictions.

And that's the problem. We're paralyzed by the infinite possibilities.

Give yourself some intentional restrictions in life and you'll finally get inspired to act.

Restrictions will set you free.

Derek Sivers (sivers.org) is a musician; the creator of CD Baby (cdbaby.com), which became the largest online seller of independent music, and the author of the bestselling book Anything You Want.

CREATIVITY-FRIENDLY CONSTRAINTS

Teresa Amabile

I have spent much of my career as a research psychologist showing how constraints can undermine creativity. But I have also discovered that the right sort of constraints can jump-start creative thinking.

Here's the key to the conundrum for managers who want to stoke the innovation fire: that close cousin of scarcity, constraint, can indeed foster creativity. Many people freeze if they are given a blank sheet of paper and told to draw something creative. But if they are given a blank sheet of paper with a squiggly line on it and asked to elaborate on that squiggle, they often have fun turning out something pretty interesting. The human mind requires stimuli—inputs for response—and certain forms of constraint serve as stimuli for creative responses.

Creativity-friendly constraints include (1) a clear problem definition with clear goals such as the specific challenges of online innovation competitions or the Iron Chef "secret ingredient" constraints and (2) a truly urgent, challenging need such as bringing the Apollo 13 astronauts safely back to earth. But intentionally strangling resources below a sufficient level in a misguided effort to spur new thinking probably will spawn only aborted attempts at innovation. The same goes for constraints that straitjacket the autonomy needed to passionately search for new solutions.

Japanese haiku, a lovely and time-honored art form, is full of tight constraints; the classic three-line poem must have five syllables, then seven syllables, then five more. But because the form offers a clear and challenging set of parameters and because there's no scarcity of words in any language, creativity can blossom.

All of which leads to a question, with apologies to the great masters of haiku:

Starving or stoking,
Scrounging or brandishing tools,
How do you create?

Teresa Amabile (progressprinciple.com) is Edsel Bryant Ford Professor of Business Administration at Harvard Business School and coauthor of The Progress Principle. *The essay here first appeared in longer form on hbr.org.*

LITTLE BETS, BIG WINS

Peter Sims

Some people swear by the "go big or go home" philosophy. If you haven't seen the movie *Moneyball,* it's about how a baseball game, which is dominated by big budgets and flashy players, can be won with the exact opposite of that way of thinking. Hitting singles and getting on base more can be a better strategy than swinging for the fences.

I learned that lesson well when I was developing my proposal for a book I wanted to write based on my work at the Stanford d.school and design thinking called *Experimental Innovation: Turning Little Bets into Breakthroughs.* Design thinking taught me the value of down and dirty prototypes, getting quick feedback, and iterating. So instead of writing a full book proposal, which is essentially a lengthy business plan for a book, I put together a three-page concept document and circulated it to a few potential "users": agents, authors, and executive readers.

I will never forget the first conversation I had with one of the agents. After I sent her my rough three-pager, she and I spoke for 30 minutes. It was a long 30 minutes and painful. I almost threw up after hanging up; it was that bad. The only thing she really liked was something in the subtitle. She liked "Little Bets."

Over a hamburger a few days later, a friend and fellow author, Ori Brafman—he wrote *Sway* and *Click*—looked at the same three-pager for about three minutes and said, "I love it! You should call this *The Little Bets Book.*" It was as if he had solved the riddle and could now eat his lunch. Then, after taking a bite, he stared into the distance with a pensive expression, turned back, and said, "I am not using little bets right now, but I should be. It's a different way of thinking."

After I moved "Little Bets" from the subtitle to the title and focused the central idea, the entire audience response suddenly changed. Nearly everyone I talked with, from agents to CEOs to friends from school to my uncle (who is a truck driver), liked the idea and found the thinking useful. Little bets with big returns was simple and to the point, and it didn't seem to matter what was in those three pages after that.

Despite the fact that I had never developed a book proposal, let alone a new book idea from scratch, "eating my own cooking," as they say, helped me not only efficiently identify the core problems but also zero in on the big idea.

If I had gone big, I might have ended up staying home.

Peter Sims (petersims.com) is a Silicon Valley–based entrepreneur and the author of Little Bets *and the coauthor of* True North. *(Photo: Nicholas Zurcher)*

ADDITION THROUGH SUBTRACTION

Seth Berkowitz

We've had to get a little crafty at audience acquisition. We don't have the brand history or the financial backing our competitors do to burn on advertising. When we huddled to build our strategy, we immediately decided to go the route of first paid search and then search engine optimization.

Our thinking was that if everyone was using Google as the gateway to the world's information, we would be more comprehensive than the rest of the pack and leverage that content girth to own access to the gateway.

We hired more journalists and data editors than everyone else and along the way generated 3.4 million pages of content. That strategy catapulted us into the top 100 most cited websites in all of Google Search and helped us build a very large audience: 17 million unique visitors a month, 100 million-plus a year. Not bad.

And yet.

Somewhere on that journey, we lost our way. In trying to do whatever it takes to help people find the car that meets their every need, we became a jack-of-all-trades and a master of none. If you want true market pricing, you can find it on our site. If you want editors' picks, you can find it on our site.

When we were completely honest with ourselves, we realized that you can find pretty similar stuff elsewhere. While we've done lots of things well, we haven't done anything that buries the rest of the pack. We haven't made them irrelevant. Not yet, anyway.

Lately, we've decided that maybe more *isn't* better. Maybe *less* is better. Less of the stuff you can get elsewhere. More of the stuff you can't. Better for our customers, better for our clients and partners, better for us. If we are going to redefine the car-buying experience in America, it will not be by providing yet more information but by making a few simple promises or guarantees and throwing all our weight behind them.

No one can foretell the future. But we're pairing our now significant weight in the automotive space with the power of subtraction in a bet that we can transform the way consumers buy cars: by removing the stress, hassle, and uncertainty inherent in the current state and restructuring the broken relationship between consumers and dealers.

The bet is on addition through subtraction.

Seth Berkowitz is the president and chief operating officer of Edmunds.com, the leading portal for automotive consumers.

FREE

Hal Macomber

December 2008. Recession situation dire. That the construction industry would be hit hard was a gross understatement. Our lean design, project management, and construction clients not only would cut back on consulting but might disappear entirely.

Our response: double down on learning and improving. But what could we offer where a fee was not a preemptive constraint? We had only one choice: leverage the limitations.

We settled on a mastermind group like that of Ben Franklin's Junto and the group of Henry Ford, Harvey Firestone, and Thomas Edison. Today, mastermind groups are generally facilitated affiliations of professional people who come together around a specific purpose, and members gladly pay to join them.

We launched the Lean Leaders Guild in March 2009 with the goal of meeting every other week for 90 minutes.

We entertained charging a small one-time fee for the year that would cover our expected costs and pay for some of our time. We tested that with some of our clients. Breaking that into a monthly charge would be easier for them. Something less than $75 might work, we thought. But after speaking to a number of prospective members, we reconsidered. We eliminated the fee entirely.

The only catch was that they had to make most of the sessions, and if they missed a session, they listened to the recordings. We pivoted away from revenue and toward contribution and participation. No easy feat in the middle of a downturn in business.

Subtracting the fee led to unexpected results. We attracted the very group of people we wanted: owners, architects, engineers, trade partners, general contractors. We developed good friendships. We attracted new business worth far more than the fees people would pay. Many of the participants started doing business with one another. Competitors teamed to pursue business. The group developed an openness to experimentation. We had very candid conversations about what was working and not working.

Free has now become a key strategy for companies. In our case, any amount we were considering charging was surely far less than the value people would derive from their participation. Subtracting that fee acknowledged that we expected to gain tremendous value from participating with them.

Free didn't just seal the deal, it ensured our success. Not only did we survive, it paved the way for us to thrive.

Hal Macomber (halmacomber.com) is practice leader at Lean Project Consulting, Inc. (leanproject. com), a Colorado-based construction management consultancy.

JACK OF ONE TRADE

Dan Schawbel

When I was starting out in my career, I took on multiple projects at once without clear goals and objectives. I really had no idea where my journey would lead to and the impact personal branding would truly have on my career.

Within six months, I had started a blog, a magazine, and a video podcast series while holding a full-time job running a Green Belt Six Sigma project and writing for online websites.

Back then, my focus was primarily on passion instead of profit. Each project I worked on limited my ability to excel at other projects that might have been more important to my future business. In a sense, I couldn't give 150 percent to the projects that would give me the best possible outcome. As a result, it took longer to grow my blog community and magazine circulation and months longer to quit my job and start a company.

Fast-forward to today, where I'm limiting and trying to justify each project that I work on with measurable objectives. Projects that I'm passionate about but don't have time for are outsourced, and I concentrate on projects that have an impact on my bottom line. I'm moving from eight websites to five websites and am consolidating my operation entirely.

I'm putting website features in place that automate my marketing systems so that I have more free time to do what's important. I've limited the services under my consulting company, and I've created a team of people who are experts in their field to help me accomplish everything. I've embraced my mistakes and learned from them and advise clients on how to avoid making them.

In some cases, the fewer projects you're involved with, the more successful you are. It's easy to spread yourself too thin when you love what you do and you see many opportunities. I get a lot of inbound queries from people who want to work with me in some capacity, and I've started turning many down. I don't consider an opportunity an opportunity when it limits your ability to have major successes in business.

It's far better to do really well at fewer things than moderately well at many things.

Dan Schawbel (danschawbel.com) is the founder of Millennial Branding and the author of Me 2.0: 4 Steps to Building Your Future.

CIRCLES OF LIFE

Moe Abdou

At the beginning of 2009, I was reading *Zen Mind, Beginner's Mind*. It really hit me about this whole eliminate piece. I realized I was spreading myself way too thin.

I decided I was going to focus on just a few things in my life. It really started with my relationships.

I sat down and drew three concentric circles. The outer circle was for acquaintances. The second was for friends. The inner circle was for the truly inspirational people in my life, the ones who if they called at 4 a.m., it would be my pleasure to help them.

It wasn't the hundreds of people in the outer circle or the 50 or 60 in that second circle but the 10 in that third inner circle who have become my focus. They have in turn had the greatest contribution to and impact on my life.

For me that simple diagram really helped direct my attention to what mattered most. It intensified my attention in the right areas and allowed me to reduce, if not eliminate, the attention I had been paying to what didn't matter anywhere near as much. I don't feel guilty anymore if someone is in that outer circle and for some reason I don't return an e-mail or phone call right away.

I did the same thing for projects I'm working on. Now I have just three key projects. Being able to say no strategically to everything else gives me the greatest opportunity to make progress on those three.

And I did it for my goals. I used to write down 20 or 30 goals at the beginning of the year that I wanted to achieve or the ideas that I wanted to devote some energy and attention to. But I never got anywhere with them. My goals now are totally different. Money didn't make it to the inner circle—it's about inspiration, it's about family, it's about relationships, it's about spirituality.

So my life is really simple: what are the three most important things for me professionally, what are my three most important goals personally, and what are the most important relationships in my life?

I've been living subtraction since 2009, and I've never been happier, more fulfilled, or more evolved.

Moe Abdou is the creator of 33voices.com, a global conversation with a mission of inspiring and igniting the ambitions of entrepreneurs everywhere.

LEVERAGING LIMITS

Paul Akers

 Two years ago our pad printing room was large, about 15 by 15 feet, with an 8-foot ceiling. In there we had a lot of tables, conveyor systems, racking, and shelving. But as our company grew and we made the decision not to buy a larger building and expand, as companies traditionally do when they grow, we asked, How can we do more with less?

Our business was growing—we launch about two dozen new products each year—and our need to pad print more products was growing, yet we didn't have the room. We challenged ourselves to cut our pad printing space in half. We found another area in our facility, half the size of the existing room, and moved the pad printing into it.

It really forced our operator to find ways to be more efficient—reduce all the resources needed, including human motion and movement, that went along with the pad printing process. He did a phenomenal job.

But we kept growing, and we now needed that half-size space for something else. Our operator found a four-foot by eight-foot by seven-foot spot underneath a pallet rack. Underneath a pallet rack!

Two years in, our sales have grown dramatically, we're pad printing much more than we used to, and now that pad printing position uses about a third of the space we started with.

I recently gave a tour of our facility, and we had three—three!—people in addition to our operator in that small space, watching the pad printing in action, cranking out hundreds of items efficiently and effectively.

How is that possible?

Simple: instead of walking from spot to spot in a nice big room, our operator sits in one spot and spins around in his swivel chair as he prints, puts the product on a conveyor belt, dries it, and drops it into a box behind him. It's a complete circle where he never has to take a step and everything has perfect flow.

That's the magic of leveraging a limit.

Paul Akers is the founder and president of FastCap, LLC (fastcap.com), a product development company based in Bellingham, Washington; host of the radio show The American Innovator *(the americaninnovator.com); and author of* 2 Second Lean.

LAW NO. 5

BREAK IS THE

IMPORTANT PART OF

BREAK*THROUGH*

Every act of creation is first of all an act of destruction.
Picasso

The first thing you notice about a Japanese-style rock garden is that little if anything actually grows in it. The second thing you notice is the nothingness of it all: a great expanse of seemingly empty space adorned with nothing more than some rather mesmerizing patterns of lines and waves in the sea gravel surrounding what appears to be randomly placed rocks. The garden is stark and simple yet elegant and beautiful.

As you gaze upon the garden, a feeling of tranquillity and serenity sweeps over you. You realize that you know that feeling; it's the one you get when you stand on the seashore at sunset, staring out at the ocean, listening to the waves crash on the shore with a natural rhythm that calms your soul. Sand, waves, water. It's a peaceful, easy feeling.

It is also the intended effect of a well-designed rock garden, and I can assure you that it is anything but easy to achieve. A number of Zen design principles work together to create that effect. For most people, though, it is the lines in the gravel that can be the most puzzling. How did they get there, who created them, and how in the world did they do that without leaving a footprint?

The Zen aesthetic ideal at play is that of *datsuzoku* (dot-soo-ZOH-koo). *Datsuzoku* is meant to denote a break—from routine, habit, or normality—to evoke the feeling of freedom from the commonplace, of transcending the ordinary and conventional, often resulting in pleasant surprise and sudden amazement. The patterned lines and grooves in the sea gravel appear to be interrupted by the rocks, but the effect is reminiscent of islands in a stream or sea and ripples in the water when a pebble is dropped. The lines may be taken to represent convention, and the rock is meant to be a surprise. *Datsuzoku* may be thought of as freedom from restriction and regulation. To a Zen practitioner, it is in the break that the seed of ultimate creativity is to be found.

When a well-worn pattern is broken, creativity emerges. It is the broken pattern that makes us sit up, take notice, and pay attention. We think differently, more resourcefully, when a break occurs.

Let's say you get a flat tire while driving. If you're normal, you curse out loud. That curse signals a break from the ordinary, which, being creatures of habit, we don't much care for. But now suddenly you're wide awake, with senses on high alert, and you're aware of a problem that requires your full attention to solve it. Suddenly everything you normally take for granted becomes vitally important: how the car handles, the shoulder of the road, safe spots to pull over, traffic around you, tire-changing tools in the trunk, immediate avenues for help. These are the resources you need for a creative solution.

They were there all along, but it was the break that brought them to your attention. Thus the fifth law of subtraction: Break *is the important part of break*through.

There are two kinds of breaks: those you make and those you take. Subtle differences to be sure, yet important enough to devote separate space to each. This chapter will look at the breaks you make, and Chapter 6 will look at those you take.

BREAKING AWAY

When it comes to healthcare, one word comes to mind: *crisis*. It's a wicked problem facing all of planet Earth. In the United States, nearly 20 percent of the gross domestic product is tied up in healthcare, nearly 50 million residents are uninsured, and those who have insurance face an average of almost $14,000 annually to cover their families as more and more employers pass greater portions of premium costs on employees or stop offering coverage entirely. Not only is it more expensive and difficult to get healthcare, the care that is delivered is far too often plagued with quality issues: there are at least 10 times more deaths caused by preventable medical errors in the United States than deaths resulting from drunk driving.* No one is happy with the system. Truly patient-centered care is a distant dream.

Or is it? Sometimes all it takes is someone willing to make a break with convention and look at the problem from a different angle.

I hadn't heard of WellnessMart, MD, until a friend told me I could get a body composition test for $10 there instead of paying $75 at my doctor's office, in addition to the fee for an office visit. I could get a full lipid profile showing my cholesterol and triglyceride levels for $45 instead of the $175 my doctor wanted to charge. I could walk in without an appointment rather than waiting three weeks to see a doctor, and I'd be done in less than five minutes.

WellnessMart is a refreshing concept: It's a cash-based retail doctor's office.

My friend did not exaggerate. Although I did spend well over an hour there, it was entirely by choice: I was talking to the founder, Dr. Richard McCauley, and chatting with him was fascinating. A graduate of the medical school at the University of Southern California, Richard had been an emergency room physician for several years before developing a new idea for healthcare.

WellnessMart looks nothing like a typical medical office. It has an attractive retail storefront, ample parking, and no waiting room. That's because there's no waiting. In fact, walking into the store feels like entering something that Apple and FedEx Office—aka Kinko's—conjured up on the back of a napkin. It's a nice mix of Apple clean and Kinko's convenience.

According to the latest statistics from the Centers for Disease Control and Prevention, just under 11,000 people die each year as a result of alcohol-impaired automobile accidents. A 1999 report by the Institute of Medicine estimated that as many as 98,000 people a year died in hospitals from medical errors. A 2010 survey from the inspector general of the Department of Health and Human Services found that about one in seven Medicare patients in hospitals suffers a serious medical mistake. The report says these adverse events contribute to the deaths of an estimated 180,000 patients a year. Among those events, roughly 80,000 are caused by errors that could be caught and prevented, such as letting infections develop, giving a patient the wrong medication, and administering an excessive dose of the right drug. The additional medical cost and care required to correct for these mistakes is estimated at more than $4 billion a year.

THE LAWS OF SUBTRACTION

Picture white and lime-green walls, modern furnishings, an open floor plan, glossy floors, big-screen televisions, and walls covered with prominent menu boards listing services and cash pricing.

"I totally copied the Apple store concept," Richard confesses. And it turns out that he's related to Kinko's founder, the business visionary Paul Orfalea—they're cousins. But what I found really intriguing was his business strategy: where in the enormous healthcare market he had chosen to play and how he planned to win.

"There are two kinds of people," states Richard. "Healthy and sick. Why do sick people and healthy people go to the same place? Every other medical site in the world treats both. We don't. We only serve healthy people. It's called 'healthcare,' not 'sick care.' Healthcare isn't just for unhealthy times. There are so many routine maintenance kinds of things you need from time to time. My sole goal in life is to make that quick, easy, and cheap."

Richard would get along just fine with the "faster, better, cheaper" crowd at NASA.

WellnessMart is a different and smarter way of doing many health-related things. You can get everything from travel shots, to tuberculosis testing, to your kids' sports-team physical. Richard can administer a multitude of medical tests, including cancer screens. You can buy physician-approved vitamins and take cardiopulmonary resuscitation (CPR) classes. It's a study in what isn't there, and the entire approach is one of subtraction: no waiting, no appointments, no old magazines, no coughs and sniffles. "If you're wheezing, sneezing, and coughing, you came to the wrong place," says Richard.

But WellnessMart can help you if you're sick. Richard and his partner, Chris Spieth, have compiled a directory showing where to get the best price on healthcare services that WellnessMart doesn't provide. You can look up where to go for doctor visits, x-rays, lab tests, dental work, and prescription drugs. They have binders containing all the information spread out on a designated table, accessible to everyone. Richard said he got the idea while working as an emergency room doctor.

"I got really frustrated working on the front lines," he tells me. "I was beginning to feel like I could never fix anything. As a physician, part of my job is to be a patient advocate within a very complex system that frustrates everybody involved. I wanted to go directly to the public—with a retail store. The idea was to create a medical marketplace with a certain level of transparency so people can see what things cost. I thought, Wouldn't it be great if healthcare was more like car care at your favorite local mechanic?"

So Richard made the break. He started small, in the hallway of a large health club, testing his concept with his potential consumer base. "Where do you find a well-contained concentration of healthy people? In a gym, working out," he says. His concept proved popular. In 2008, he launched WellnessMart in a small strip mall in Thousand Oaks, California, a suburb of Los Angeles. His break is now officially consolidated: he has two stores in northern California's Sacramento area and another in West Los Angeles, for a total of four.

But Richard's solution doesn't stop at health maintenance. He's tackling the toughest and most opaque part of healthcare: insurance. WellnessMart is a cash business and doesn't take insurance, but it sells policies and educates people on insurance. "Health insurance should really be more like car insurance," he says. "You buy car insurance for accidents, not for oil changes, tune-ups, and tires. You don't go to Jiffy Lube and hand them your insurance card, right? But that's how health insurance operates. It's ludicrous. If car insurance companies tried to sell policies the way health insurance companies do—five times more expensive than they should be and partially paying for routine maintenance—nobody would buy them."

Richard wants people to look at health insurance the way they look at auto and home insurance: as something to purchase for the big disasters. "People should be buying health insurance strictly for the unexpected crisis," he says. "There is so much savings there. A deductible in your car insurance is straightforward—if something happens, you pay the deductible and the insurance company handles the rest. Not so in health insurance. In all but a few cases, you keep paying. It's a different concept but the same word. And it's not right."

He educated me about my own health insurance and on the value of a healthcare savings account. He showed me how to save thousands of dollars by simply shifting my understanding of what insurance is and what it isn't. With this philosophy, the money I can save in premiums pays for the services I actually use, tax-free through a health savings account.

Richard is a licensed insurance broker, but he recommends and sells only a few catastrophic policies. He showed me a number of different plans, ran different scenarios on them, and easily illustrated how just a few were worthwhile because they operated more like auto insurance.

WellnessMart represents a profound improvement for consumers: a place they can walk into and get honest answers. "Let's live in the real world where people have limited resources. Not everybody can afford everything," Richard tells me. "If people can get the same quality of care for less money, let's start there and give people the opportunity to experience healthcare in a positive way. Let's allow them to ask questions and learn. Traditional medical offices are not set up to teach. They're set up to diagnose and treat."

That's another cue Richard took from an Apple store: the notion of a "genius bar." Each WellnessMart store has an educational area equipped with large screens and ample seating. Training classes regularly teach CPR, first aid, and child safety. I found the entire concept and the experience to be one of the most effective I'd ever encountered. I asked Richard if he plans to expand nationally or perhaps franchise. "We are staying small and lean right now," he says. But he's well positioned to take advantage of what appears to be a growing opportunity: the National Center for Policy Analysis in Dallas expects the number of walk-in clinics to almost triple in the next four years in response to patient demand.

"You know that 2,500-page healthcare reform act working its way through Congress?" Richard asks. "All you need is one sentence: 'Healthcare service providers must openly post the price of every service on a menu.' Problem solved, game over. We have to break with convention, and that's how to do it. That's how we did it."

As I walked away, I couldn't help thinking that I had just realized my first victory over healthcare issues. For $10, I got a body composition profile, an education in how to simplify the most complex situations, and advice on how to save tens of thousands of dollars. I knew I'd be back. Again and again.

BREAKING BARRIERS

If you head north from Los Angeles on Interstate 5, hang a right on the Antelope Valley Freeway toward Palmdale and the Mojave Desert, and cut east past the Antelope Valley Country Club, you'll run into the Sierra Highway, off which you can see Lockheed Martin's Skunk Works building, not far from Air Force Plant 42 and Edwards Air Force Base. You'll know you're in the right place because you'll see a white building with a cartoon skunk on it: the Skunk Works logo. As you drive around, you'll see a good bit of barbed wire, a high concrete wall, and plenty of "No Access" signs. You'll see an F-104 Starfighter on display near the main entrance off Lockheed Way and pass Kelly's Way, named for Lockheed's legendary chief engineer, Clarence "Kelly" Johnson.

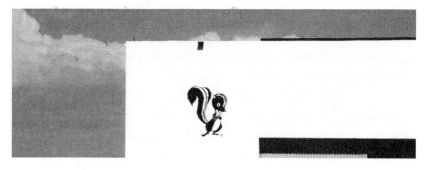

Image source: Wikimedia Commons.

No matter how hard you try or how many times you call the Lockheed Martin public relations office, you will not get inside; that is, unless you ask about a fairly obscure program such as the Advanced Composite Cargo Aircraft. You'll then be invited to take a tour of the project hangar.* Skunk Works is, and has been since its inception under Kelly during World War II, Lockheed's top-secret Advanced Development Program.

---

* *In March 2009, the blogger Steve Trimble, who writes the DEW (Defense Early Warning) Line blog for the aviation site flightglobal.com, did just that. After many unsuccessful direct attempts, he asked for a phone interview with the program manager of the Advanced Composite Cargo Aircraft and immediately was granted access. I, however, had no such luck.*

Kelly Johnson ran Lockheed's innovative Skunk Works for nearly 45 years, from its inception in 1943 to 1975, when he turned the reins over to his longtime right-hand man, friend, and protégé, Ben "Stealth" Rich, who ran it until 1991, when he retired from Lockheed after over 40 years of service.*

Skunk Works was not always situated out in the middle of the desert, and it did not always have its own building. In fact, when it began, it had no building at all. The Skunk Works story begins in World War II and is a tale of one world-changing aviation breakthrough after another at the hands of departure from convention. As in the stories of Pathfinder and Lexus, it is the enormous complexity of the work, the superb design quality, the limited resources, and the radical thinking with which those breakthroughs were achieved that make the Skunk Works story worth retelling.

It was the appearance of Germany's first jet fighter planes in the skies over Europe that prompted the U.S. War Department in 1943 to knock on the door of Lockheed Aircraft Corporation, headquartered in Burbank, California, next to the Burbank airport. Lockheed actually owned the airport and had gone to great lengths to conceal the entire area from Japanese air reconnaissance. An enormous burlap tarp painted to depict a suburban neighborhood camouflaged the factory, adorned with artificial trees, buildings, and cars (made of rubber) to give it a three-dimensional effect.

For the War Department, there was just one man for the job: 33-year-old Kelly Johnson, Lockheed's talented but eccentric chief engineer.

In his memoir *Skunk Works*, Ben Rich described Kelly as always "rushing around in his untucked shirt" with "a comical duck's waddle, slicked-down white hair, and a belligerent jaw." According to Ben, Kelly looked like W. C. Fields, complete with a thick, round nose but without the humor.

"Definitely without that," Ben wrote. "Johnson was all business and had the reputation of an ogre who ate young, tender engineers for between-meal snacks. We peons viewed him with the knee-knocking dread and awe

---

* *Ben Rich ushered in the era of stealth fighter design for Lockheed's Skunk Works. When he passed away in January 1995, his ashes were spread from a plane in the skies over the Pacific Ocean near his home in southern California at his request. Just as his ashes were released, a stealth fighter suddenly emerged from the clouds, dipped its wings in a final salute to its creator, and vanished as suddenly as it had appeared.*

of the Almighty best described in the Old Testament. The guy would just as soon fire you as have to chew on you for some goof-up. Right or not, that was the lowdown on Kelly Johnson. But the open secret in our company was that the chief engineer walked on water in the adoring eyes of CEO Robert Gross."

It was Robert Gross who saved Lockheed from extinction by buying it out of bankruptcy in 1932 for the tidy sum of $40,000. Gross risked everything by placing his money on the development of a twin-engine commercial airplane. During wind tunnel tests at the University of Michigan, a 23-year-old engineering student of Swedish descent by the name of Clarence Johnson contradicted his professors and told Lockheed engineers that their design was seriously flawed: if one engine went out, the plane would go down.

Lockheed hired Johnson for his audacity, and before long he was nicknamed "Kelly" for his "fighting Irish" temper. Not only did Kelly correct the design flaw, he did so with an unconventional twin-tail design that would become the Lockheed signature. The plane, the Electra, saved Lockheed and revolutionized aviation in the 1930s. Kelly's star rose, and he became the go-to guy on everything from aerodynamics to flight testing, including flying the planes he built; he declared that unless he scared himself nearly to death once a year in a cockpit, he wouldn't have the proper perspective to design good planes. That's *genchi genbutsu* at its finest.

Kelly was a maverick and often left people in his wake. "Once that guy made up his mind to do something," Ben Rich writes, "he was as relentless as a bowling ball heading toward a ten-pin strike. With his chili-pepper temperament, he was poison to any bureaucrat, a disaster to ass-coverers, excuse-makers, or fault-finders."

Kelly took all of three days in the late 1930s to transform the Electra into a bomber for the British Royal Air Force. Called the Hudson, it was so successful that England ordered 3,000. Kelly's colleagues were so awestruck by his design skills that they swore he could actually see air.

In 1939 Kelly designed and built the only American fighter plane in production throughout U.S. involvement in World War II: the P-38 Lightning Interceptor. If you've seen World War II footage, you've seen the P-38. It's the twin-propeller plane with the funny-looking twin-boom tail design.

It was the most maneuverable propeller plane of the war and played several roles: ground attack, air-to-air combat, and strategic bombing. It was the P-38 that not only shot down Japanese Admiral Isoruku Yamamoto's airplane but also was responsible for shooting down more Japanese aircraft than any other fighter plane during the war.

As with the Mars Pathfinder and the Lexus LS400, challenging constraints shaped the project: build a jet fighter prototype that would fly at 600 miles per hour—the edge of the speed of sound and 200 miles per hour faster than the P-38—in 180 days. The only problem was that Lockheed was out of floor space, as the entire complex was devoted to 24/7 production of the current planes.

The jet fighter project was to be conducted with top secrecy, and so the space constraint was something Kelly decided to leverage. He rented a large circus tent, borrowed 23 of the best design engineers and 30 shop mechanics from Lockheed's main operation, and set up camp next to a foul-smelling plastics factory, figuring that the overwhelming odor would help keep "nosy barkers" away.

The whole setup reminded people of Al Capp's *L'il Abner* comic strip and the "Skonk Works," a dilapidated factory on the remote outskirts of Capp's fictional backwoods town, Dogpatch, run by one Big Barnsmell, the lonely "inside man." In Capp's comics, scores of Dogpatch locals are done in every year by the toxic fumes of concentrated "skonk oil," which Big and his cousin Barney brewed and barreled daily by grinding dead skunks and worn shoes into a constantly smoldering still for a purpose that Capp never disclosed.

"The connection was apparent to those inside Kelly's circus tent forced to suffer the plastic factory's stink," writes Ben. "One day one of the engineers showed up for work wearing a civil defense gas mask as a gag, and a designer named Irv Culver picked up a ringing phone and announced, 'Skonk Works.'"

The name stuck, and behind Kelly's back his team began referring to the operation as "the Skonk Works." It wasn't long before even those working at the main Lockheed plant were calling it that too. Over the next 15 years, Skonk Works became part of the Lockheed lexicon. In 1960, when Al Capp's publisher objected to Lockheed's use of the name, rather than abandon it, Lockheed changed it to Skunk Works and registered both the name and the cartoon skunk logo as trademarks, thus becoming the official alias of the Lockheed Advanced Development Program.

Over the years, the term *skunk works* has come to refer to any effort involving an elite special team that breaks away from the larger organization to work autonomously on an advanced or secret project, usually tasked with breakthrough innovation on limited budgets and under aggressive timelines. The term has become official and is defined in the fourth edition of the *American Heritage Dictionary of the English Language* as "an often secret experimental laboratory or facility for producing innovative products, as in the computer or aerospace field."

Perhaps it was the stink that drove Kelly's secret team to design and build the prototype for the P-80 Shooting Star—nicknamed Lulu Belle—in a mere 143 days, 37 days ahead of schedule. Although World War II ended before the jet fighter could prove itself, Lockheed produced nearly 9,000 during the lead-up to the Korean War. The P-80, later called the F-80, won the first all-jet dogfight over the skies above North Korea, shooting down a Soviet MiG-15 and becoming the first American jet fighter to score a kill.

Given the success of the P-80 project, Lockheed management agreed to let Kelly keep his elite design and development team running as long as it did not interfere in any way with Kelly's primary duties as Lockheed's chief engineer and was kept on a shoestring budget. Kelly hand-selected a few of the brightest designers and moved into a building known only as Building 82. Skunk Works would remain there until it moved operations out to the desert in Palmdale in 1994. Kelly split his time between the main Lockheed plant and Building 82, usually turning his attention to Skunk Works in the later part of the day.

"Those guys brainstormed what-if questions about the future needs of commercial and military aircraft," Ben writes, "and if one of their ideas resulted in a contract to build an experimental prototype, Kelly would borrow the best people he could find in the main plant to get the job done. That way the overhead was kept low and the financial risks to the company stayed small."

There was nothing fancy about the Skunk Works space. In fact, Kelly preferred to keep things as spare as possible. When Ben Rich was lent out temporarily to Kelly in 1954, little did he know that he'd never leave. He describes his first impression of the space as being nearly as eccentric as Kelly himself:

> The office space allocated to Kelly's Skunk Works operation was a narrow hallway off the main production floor crowded with drilling machines and presses, small parts assemblies, and the large assembly area which served as the production line. There were two floors of surprisingly primitive and overcrowded offices where about fifty designers and engineers were jammed together behind as many desks as a moderate-size room could unreasonably hold. Space was at a premium, so much so that Kelly's ten-person procurement department operated from a small balcony looking down on the production floor. The place was airless and gloomy and had the look of a temporary campaign headquarters where all the chairs and desks were rented and disappeared the day after the vote.
>
> But there was no sense of imminent eviction apparent inside Kelly's Skunk Works. His small group was all young and high-spirited, who thought nothing of working out of a phone booth, if necessary, as long as they were designing and building airplanes. Added to the eccentric flavor of the place was the fact that when the hangar doors were opened, birds would fly up the stairwell and swoop around drawing boards and dive-bomb our heads, after knocking themselves silly against the permanently sealed and blacked-out windows, which Kelly insisted upon for security. Our little feathered friends were a real nuisance, but Kelly couldn't care less. All that mattered to him was our proximity to the production floor. A stone's throw was too far away; he wanted us only steps away from the shop workers, to make quick structural or parts changes or answer any of their questions.

That first secret project set the standard for every Skunk Works project to follow, including the U-2 bomber, the SR-71 Blackbird, and the F-117 Nighthawk stealth fighter. High-quality designs in a short time with limited resources became the hallmark of a Skunk Works project.

Kelly had three simple management principles supporting a single fundamental belief: don't build an airplane you don't believe in. His three principles: First, it's more important to listen than to talk; second, even a timely wrong decision is better than no decision; and third, don't halfheartedly wound problems—kill them dead.

Over time, Kelly developed 14 rules for all Skunk Works projects as a way to put his core belief and basic principles into practice. Half of the rules (with a few word changes) can be applied to any skunk works project, and they prescribe a robust framework within which to operate:

- The Skunk Works manager must be delegated practically complete control of his program in all aspects. He should report to a division president or higher.

- Strong but small project offices must be provided.*

- The number of people having any connection with the project must be restricted in an almost vicious manner. Use a small number of good people (10% to 25% compared to the so-called normal systems).

- A very simple drawing and drawing release system with great flexibility for making changes must be provided.

- There must be a minimum number of reports required, but important work must be recorded thoroughly.

- The contractor must be delegated the authority to test his final product in flight. He can and must test it in the initial stages. If he doesn't, he rapidly loses his competence to design other vehicles.

- Access by outsiders to the project and its personnel must be strictly controlled by appropriate security measures.

---

* *The full rule reads "both by the military and industry." The remaining seven rules are all specifically focused on Lockheed work and military defense contract work. You can see all 14 at lockheedmartin.com/us/aeronautics/skunkworks/14rules.html.*

Ben Rich neatly tied together the elements that have allowed the Skunk Works program to enjoy an ongoing record of breakthrough innovation for nearly 70 years:

> We created a practical and open work environment for engineers and shop workers, forcing the guys behind the drawing boards onto the shop floor to see how their ideas were being translated into actual parts and to make any necessary changes on the spot. We made every shop worker who designed or handled a part responsible for quality control. Any worker—not just a supervisor or a manager—could send back a part that didn't meet his or her standards. That way we reduced rework and scrap waste.
>
> We encouraged our people to work imaginatively, to improvise and try unconventional approaches to problem solving, and then got out of their way. By applying the most common-sense methods to develop new technologies, we saved tremendous amounts of time and money while operating in an atmosphere of trust and cooperation both with our government customers and between our white-collar and blue-collar employees.
>
> In the end, Lockheed's Skunk Works demonstrated the awesome capabilities of American inventiveness when free to operate under near ideal working conditions. That may be our most enduring legacy as well as our source of lasting pride. A successful Skunk Works will always demand a strong leader and a work environment dominated by highly motivated employees. The Skunk Works' strength is the autonomy they have enjoyed from management and their close teamwork and partnership with their customers. . . .

If you're contemplating your own skunk works project, take a page from Kelly Johnson and Lockheed's Skunk Works.

SKUNK WORK

The Macintosh division of Apple Computer began as a small skunk works project for a low-cost computer that was being developed by Apple employee Jef Raskin. It was Raskin who introduced Steve Jobs to Xerox Palo Alto Research Center (PARC) engineers who had developed the graphical user interface technology that would one day become the hallmark of Apple Computer's operating system.

In his book *Steve Jobs*, biographer Walter Isaacson tells how in 1979 Raskin wrote a manifesto titled *Computers by the Millions*, whose opening lines read: "If personal computers are to be truly personal, it will have to be as likely as not that a family, picked at random, will own one." It was thus Raskin's vision, not Steve Jobs's, of a "computer for the masses" built to be essentially an inexpensive, self-contained appliance using a graphical interface. Raskin got permission to begin a small development project, which he named after his favorite kind of apple, the McIntosh, changing the spelling to avoid confusion with the name of the high-fidelity sound system company McIntosh Laboratory.

Raskin and Jobs didn't see eye to eye, and Raskin left Apple. By that time, Jobs had been stripped of his research and development role and made the nonexecutive chairman of the board, without operational control. Since it was a minor project, Jobs was allowed to take over the Raskin Macintosh project, which suited Apple management fine: it kept Jobs occupied in a distant building away from the main operation. It suited Jobs as well: "It was like going back to the garage for me," he told Isaacson. "I had my own ragtag team and I was in control."

Jobs cherry-picked a team of about 20 "pirates," as he referred to them, and seceded from the Apple main campus. He relocated the team to a small building three blocks away, next to a Texaco station. The two-story brown-shingled building became known as Texaco Towers.

(continues)

(continued)

The saga of Steve Jobs and Macintosh began as a breaking away. When the Mac came out, it was incompatible with both of the existing Apple products: Apple II and the Lisa. It would soon eclipse them and become the mainstay of the Apple line.

As the success of Macintosh grew, so did the team, becoming a division, and it moved back to the main Apple campus in 1983. Jobs kept the renegade spirit alive with his maxim "It's better to be a pirate than join the navy." Jobs actively recruited rebels and swashbucklers—talented but audacious individuals who could move fast and get things done—to his A Team.

On his twenty-eighth birthday, programmer Steve Capps hoisted a Jolly Roger with the Apple logo for an eye patch, and the team erected a billboard outside Apple headquarters that read: "Happy 28th, Steve. The Journey Is the Reward—The Pirates."

BREAKING FREE

The mysteries of the mind and brain are many and complex. Neuroscience, through the magic of technology, is just beginning to unravel some of them. In light of the fact that my livelihood revolves around creativity and change—in fact, creating change—I am a voracious consumer of all things neuro. I'm especially fascinated by neuroplasticity.

Neuroplasticity is the ability of the mind to change the brain. Yes, you read that right. Neuroplasticity radically reverses ages of scientific dogma holding that mental experiences result only from physical goings-on in the brain and that we can't do much about that. The brain is the brain, or so the thinking went, and it doesn't change once it's hardwired, and even if it did, it couldn't possibly be a person's thoughts that were responsible. But neuroscience can now confirm that our mental machinations *do* alter the physical structure of our brain matter. Thus, when you change your mind, you change your brain.

This is great news for most of us, because the universal issue facing everyone in this age of excessive complexity is *change,* whether it's breaking a habit, adopting a new one, coming up with new and original ideas, shifting a business focus, changing behaviors, changing company culture, or changing the world. At the heart of the matter is the issue of breaking out of well-grooved patterns—minds and mindsets—and creating new ones; in other words, unlocking the brain.

I first met Dr. Jeffrey Schwartz, a practicing neuropsychiatrist affiliated with UCLA, in 2008. Jeff is the author of several books, including *You Are Not Your Brain, The Mind and the Brain,* and *Brain Lock.* What's interesting about Jeff is that he deals with one of the most prevalent, challenging, and debilitating patterns in the brain: obsessive-compulsive disorder (OCD). He's an internationally recognized authority who developed a successful behavioral therapy at UCLA's medical school for patients with OCD, called the "UCLA Four Steps."

And here's the thing: he doesn't use drugs to treat patients. He teaches them to reset and rewire their brains by changing the way they think.

If anyone knows about the pattern-making, pattern-recognizing, pattern-locking machine that is the human brain, it's Jeff Schwartz. "Your brain is like a DVR," says Jeff. "It records every sensory experience you have and sends that information to your frontal cortex, which houses your brain's higher functions, and stores it as data. The process is ongoing, and there is no real editing that goes on. An automatic grouping mechanism gets triggered when new information comes in, so the new information gets filed with other like data. That's how your brain creates specific and unique patterns. Different patterns combine to make memories and perceptions. Those connections are reinforced over time and quickly become mental models—mindsets, if you will."

Those mental models allow us to function, for the most part, much more efficiently and effectively by helping us rapidly sift data and sort information into useful knowledge according to whether it confirms or contradicts the strong patterns already embedded in the brain.

OCD occurs when a good brain pattern—such as washing one's hands—goes bad: it gets chained, locked, and encrypted by the brain like a steel vault. The pattern is amazingly robust and resistant to change. "OCD is an insatiable monster," Jeff says. "The more you give it, the hungrier it gets. Even Howard Hughes, with all his wealth, with a retinue of servants to perform the bizarre rituals his OCD told him to perform, couldn't buy his way out. Eventually, the false messages coming from his brain overwhelmed him."

OCD is related to chemical imbalances in the brain and is a lifelong disease identified by two groups of symptoms: obsessions and compulsions. Obsessions are intrusive, unwelcome, distressing thoughts and mental images. They don't go away by themselves. Jeff refers to this as "brain lock" because connections between parts of the brain get locked together, leaving a person unable to shift from one thought to the next. Compulsions are the behaviors OCD sufferers perform in a vain attempt to exorcise the fears and anxieties caused by their obsessions. What Jeff has proved is that his OCD patients can change how they respond to their obsessions by using their thoughts to physically change the way their brains work; in other words, by exploiting the brain's neuroplasticity.

When you look at a brain scan of someone with OCD and compare it with a scan of a normal brain, you notice that the OCD brain is all lit up—highly and abnormally overactive in places where the normal brain isn't. The cortex of the OCD brain, which is where the messages from other areas are connected and become thought, is where all the action is. Specifically, it's in what is called the orbital cortex, which is like an error-detection unit, a sort of "check engine" light. After a successful treatment using the four-step cognitive behavior therapy, that area of an OCD patient's brain shows a nearly miraculous decrease in activity, leaving it closer to normal. Showing this type of imagery to OCD patients is a critical step, because they understand from the start that it's not *them*, it's their *brains* that have a few glitches and that they can change their brains to manage those glitches.

This separation enables the therapy to begin working by invoking the belief system. It's when we *believe* we can make a break that we break through whatever barriers are holding us in place. This is the reason I am drawn to Jeff's work in the first place. It's not because I'm curious about OCD per se but because of what he knows about breaking free of those kinds of fiercely strong patterns. If his method helps people with OCD, doesn't it make sense that we should be able to use it in making any kind of change?

As he described the four steps to me, the answer became obvious: Yes.

1. Relabel

"The first step is to relabel a given thought, feeling, or behavior as something else," Jeff says. "An unwanted thought could be relabeled 'false message' or 'brain glitch.' This amounts to training yourself to clearly recognize and identify what is real and what isn't, refusing to be tricked by your own intrusive thoughts and urges. Essentially you call the thought or urge exactly what it is: an obsessive thought or a compulsive urge. For someone with OCD, instead of saying, 'I have to check the stove,' they would start saying, 'I'm having a compulsive urge to check the stove.'"

Now, in order to do this, notice that you are really engaging in a bit of personal subtraction and *genchi genbutsu*: you are removing yourself from the equation and *observing* yourself objectively. "I bring out the impartial spectator," Jeff explains.

Adam Smith in his 1759 treatise *The Theory of Moral Sentiments* defined "the impartial and well-informed spectator" as the ability to stand outside of oneself and watch "the person within" in action. "We each have access to this person, and that's what you learn to do in the relabel step," says Jeff. "You step back and say, 'This is just my brain sending me a false message; if I change my behavior, my brain will change.'"

This sounds easy, almost a trite affirmation, like what they give you at one of those weekend-long shut-in sessions where you transform yourself into the person you always thought you could be. It isn't. It's hard. Adam Smith knew how hard it could be to do this, writing that it requires the "utmost and most fatiguing exertion." The reason isn't hard to figure out: when your brain is sending rapid-fire, long-embedded directions at you with overwhelming force, focusing on something completely different is incredibly difficult.

2. Reattribute

The second step is to reattribute, which answers a key question that Jeff poses: "Why do these thoughts come back? The answer is that the brain is misfiring, stuck in gear, creating mental noise, and sending false messages. In other words, if you understand why you're getting those old thoughts, eventually you'll be able to say, 'Oh, that's just my OCD, or that's just a brain glitch.'" That raises the next question: What can you do about it?

3. Refocus

The third step is to refocus, and this is where the toughest work is, because it entails the actual changing of behavior. You have to do another behavior instead of the old one. Having recognized the problem for what it is and understood why it's occurring, you now have to replace the old behavior with new, more constructive things to do. This is where the change in brain chemistry occurs, because you are cutting new grooves, new patterns, new mindsets.

By refusing to be misled by the old messages, by understanding they aren't what they tell you they are, you find that your mind is now in charge of your brain. This is basically like shifting the gears of a car manually. "The automatic transmission isn't working, so you manually override it," says Jeff. "With positive, desirable alternatives—gardening, riding a bike, anything you enjoy and can do consistently each and every time—you are actually repairing the gearbox. The more you do it, the smoother the shifting becomes. Like most other things, the more you practice, the more easy and natural it becomes, because your brain is beginning to function more efficiently, calling up the new pattern without thinking about it."

4. Revalue

It all comes together in the fourth step, which is the natural outcome of the first three. With a consistent way to replace the old behavior with the new, you begin to see old patterns as simple distractions. You devalue them as being completely worthless. Eventually the thoughts and urges begin to fade in intensity, the brain works better and better, and the automatic transmission in the brain starts working properly.

"Two very positive things happen," Jeff says. "The first is that you're happier, because you have control over your behavioral response to your thoughts and feelings. The second thing is that by doing that, you change the faulty brain chemistry."

Jeff confirms that his methods can be used to create change in any area of business, work, or life. "Since it has been scientifically demonstrated that the brain has been altered through the behavior change," he says, "it's safe to say that you could do the same thing by altering responses to any number of other behaviors."

What all of this meant to me was that we can learn to improve our ability to defeat the traditional thinking traps we fall into when we try to change our view of whatever challenge we're facing. We can override our default. We can retrain our brains by exercising the Apple tagline: Think different.

The UCLA Four Steps group gained world acclaim, and the success raised deeper questions for Jeff: What happens at the instant a person decides not to check the stove after decades of doing it in response to her brain's false signals and in spite of her racing heart and churning gut? What is responsible for her ability to suddenly switch gears, activating other circuitry?

That would be important for anyone who is at least somewhat mentally paralyzed to understand. "At the instant of activation," Jeff says, "both circuits are ready to go—one encoding your walk out the door for a jog, the other a rush back to the stove. Yet something in the mind is choosing one brain circuit over the other. Something is causing one to activate, the other to stay quiet. What *is* that something?"

The renowned psychology pioneer William James was seeking an answer to that question over a hundred years ago when he asked "by what process is it that the thought of any given action comes to prevail stably in the mind?"

For Jeff, these questions launched a new immersion in the study of how the mind can change the brain. What was accounting for the observed changes in the physical brain? Good old-fashioned willpower was the most reasonable explanation. But this went against the theory many scientists still labored under, a purely reductionist view that the mind is simply a result of brain stuff—implying that conscious thought couldn't possibly change actual brain hardware. For the first time, "mind over matter" had hard science behind it. Jeff had the solid evidence from brain imaging that a change had taken place, and he believed that a directed mental force accounted for it. You can imagine the old-schoolers saying, "It's all just one part of the brain changing another, it's still the brain doing it all on its own, don't bring the conscious mind into it." But the successful treatment of OCD patients required tapping into the belief that they had power over their actions. That's how behavioral therapy works.

What Jeff was able to show was that the mind, through a directed mental force, can activate one brain circuit over another, and once the new circuit begins to fire on a regular basis, you need *less* force to activate it. In other words, the relabeling and refocusing of attention start becoming automatic. As the brain takes over the heavy lifting, the mind resets.

The neuroscience of change reveals the power behind the fifth law of subtraction: Breakthrough often demands that one simply make a conscious break from existing routines and patterns and then stick with it.

It's the sticking with it part, though, that has yet another dimension and quite possibly is the key to tapping one's most creative self.

SILHOUETTES

IN SUBTRACTION

Jonathan Fields

Michael Bungay Stanier

Tanner Christensen

Karen Martin

Robert Morris

Bruce Rosenstein

Dan Keldsen

Jamie Flinchbaugh

Brian Buck

SAVE THE BUTTERFLIES

Jonathan Fields

I gave up a seven-figure income as a lawyer to make $12 an hour as a personal trainer. Crazy, right? Then, married and with a three-month-old baby, I signed a lease to launch a yoga center in the heart of Hell's Kitchen in New York City the day before 9/11. Forget crazy; it was utter insanity.

Not only did I survive, I flourished and prospered. Along the way, I learned some real-life lessons that enabled me to develop a fresh approach to transforming uncertainty, risk of loss, and exposure to judgment into catalysts for innovation, creation, and achievement.

I'm learning to become a fear alchemist. Fear alchemists are people who have spent some time understanding the process and experience of fear, what it is and what it isn't, and then equipped themselves with the strategies, skills, and tools to take that experience and instead of having it paralyze them, turn it into something that mobilizes them. I'm an aspiring one, still exploring, but I've learned a thing or two.

First, it helps to have some "certainty anchors": things that you can count on, that you know recur regularly, every day, in your life in a fairly automated way. You can look forward to them always being the same, always being there. The power of a certainty anchor is that it gives you a sort of baseline calm—ropes to the ground, if you will—so that you feel more comfortable going to that untethered creative place where you really just let go. Certainty anchors assure you that you'll still be able to touch back down after blasting off.

The question for many people is, How do you minimize or avoid the collateral damage—to other parts of your life and others in your life—in chasing your creative passion if it's something dramatically different from your current path?

Easy: build something on the side. Do it as a skunk works. Do it in your spare time. Take the four-plus hours the average Joe spends watching mindless TV and do something with it. People say, "I need that time to wind down." Baloney. When you're doing something you're passionate about, it energizes you. At some point, if you keep at it, you can make the break to the new path when the new idea is viable. Meantime, you keep your responsibilities and provide the security and stability those in your life rely on.

There is something you never, ever want to remove: butterflies. If you kill the butterflies in your stomach, you'll kill the dream. Most people back away when they get that nervous, uncomfortable feeling. But that feeling signals that you're doing something that matters to you. Embrace the feeling. Try to understand what the feeling is telling you. Train yourself in the alchemy of fear. Save the butterflies.

Jonathan Fields (jonathanfields.com) is the author most recently of Uncertainty: Turning Fear and Doubt into Fuel for Brilliance.

LESS ADVICE, MORE CURIOSITY

Michael Bungay Stanier

 You're on the quest for elegance, for focus, for impact. And yet overwhelm is forever tapping on your shoulder. More meetings to attend, more e-mails to process, more projects to manage, more dotted lines to and from, more plates to spin, more people with whom to connect. And that's just at work.

Our natural reaction is to speed things up: refine our processes and get more and more efficient, rush to get things done, find the answer, and create an action plan that gets things moving.

But an elegant solution to the wrong problem is not an elegant solution.

It's a simple, powerful, and rare discipline to take just a little more time at the front end to figure out what the real challenge might be. There are a few things that help me do more of what matters and less of the rest.

First, I slow down. It's my impatience as much as anyone else's that's got me rushing to the solution. I take a breath and decide I'm going to give myself time just to be curious about what's really going on.

I refuse to be seduced by the presenting challenge. I have a working hypothesis that the first thing that comes up is most likely not the real thing, just an interesting starting point. The first thing that comes out of someone's mouth is rarely the real thing. It's often a best guess, or a smoke screen, or even a solution to the unarticulated challenge. And by "someone" I'm talking as much about me as I am about a person I might be talking to.

I turn off my advice-giving machine. I just love to help. I want to add value. I want them to help me help them, like Jerry Maguire. But if I'm giving advice, I'm already down the path of action and complexity. It's hard to be curious when you're telling someone what to do.

More questions. Less advice. That's my mantra. But what questions? Here's the one that makes the difference: What's the real challenge here?

That question alone will add focus to everything and for everyone. If I really want to amp up my curiosity muscle, I'll add this question to the mix: And what else? Asking that acknowledges that the first thing someone says is not the only thing that person has in mind and probably not even the best or most important thing. It's a self-management tool to stop me from jumping into action. It keeps me in curiosity mode.

From curiosity comes insight, from insight comes clarity, and from clarity comes elegant and focused action.

Michael Bungay Stanier (boxofcrayons.biz) is the senior partner of Box of Crayons and the author of Do More Great Work *and the philanthropic* End Malaria.

AN INSPIRING EMPTINESS

Tanner Christensen

An apartment that was empty except for a plain camping mat was my life when I first moved to Salt Lake City some years ago.

Whenever friends came over to visit, they were astonished at the void that was my living space. Whereas the typical living arrangement for anyone in his or her early twenties consisted of a large TV, posters on the walls, video game consoles, and a messy bed or at the very least an unkempt mattress, my apartment was completely empty.

Can you imagine living without the comfort of a coffee machine, a TV, a bookshelf, even a dresser drawer for clothes?

For more than a year I got by exceptionally well without any major belongings, and I did it for a good reason.

At the time my life was dedicated to my work, to writing and creating a remarkable—albeit small—e-book publishing house. The way I saw it, a television or a couch or an excessive collection of books could inspire me but, more important, could work as a distraction as well.

So I went without.

And for the first time in my life I found myself immensely inspired by my own means. Day and night I would focus my energies on creating my own inspiration and pushing my business ideas forward. When friends came over to visit, we would either sip wine and talk about how we were going to change the world—which worked marvelously as a motivational tool—or gather scraps of paper and canvas and paint or draw to our hearts' content.

I was essentially living without anything that didn't push me to pursue my dreams and goals. If you have never seen the photo of Steve Jobs in his home in California at the age of 23, only a lamp and a rug filling the large space around him, it's worth finding and looking at.

Steve Jobs knew, as I knew when I moved to the city, that removing elements from your life that don't directly relate to your goals or essential survival can be remarkably inspirational and motivating.

If you're looking for a good boost in productivity and want to change your life, start by removing what you don't really need. It's certainly not easy to do, but it can work remarkably well as a way to start doing the things you need to and engaging your imagination.

Tanner Christensen (tannerchristensen.com) is the founder of the e-book publisher Aspindle.com.

FEAR NOT

Karen Martin

For me, subtraction is about uncluttering, removing the obstacles, and letting go of burdens that stand between the way things are and the way you want them to be in the future. I've come to realize that before you can remove any burden you carry, you need to let go of why you're carrying it in the first place: fear.

Rational fear is a good thing, as it alerts us to potential danger. But irrational fear is a different beast. It's what causes us to hold on to burdens we should really remove. When I reflect on the accomplishments that I'm most proud of, removing fear was always step one. The best example I have is when I decided to leave my job and launch my own business in the middle of a promotion to vice president.

I had always dreamed of running my own business. But each time I got close to making the leap, the fear of jumping into deep water kept me on the ship. Could I make it financially? Why leave the great compensation and big title behind? On the surface, all my questions revolved around money and prestige. Or did they?

On the Friday afternoon before the Monday I was to start, I met with my boss, the COO, to finalize everything. I left the meeting feeling empty instead of elated, which puzzled me. I liked my job, team, and leadership. But something wasn't right. I knew what I had to do to sort out my conflicted feelings: deep reflection.

That weekend was the most difficult and most profound I've ever had. I closed my blinds and turned off the phone. I thought and thought and then thought some more. And I *felt*. The more I imagined life as a solo consultant, the more excited I got. And then at noon on Sunday, it finally hit me. My fear wasn't about money and title per se; it was how I had come to view money and title as the very definition of success. This aha moment was the most liberating experience I've ever had. The moment I gained clarity about my fear, it lost all its power.

On Monday morning, I resigned. Saying good-bye wasn't easy. I had been the first employee hired, and I had put my heart and soul into that company. And now I was taking them back.

Nineteen years later, the warning our COO gave me—"you'll hate consulting"—hasn't panned out. Quite the opposite. Subtracting fear from the equation opened up a wonderful world of possibilities that keeps getting better.

I can now smell fear. And I can help others let go of the clutter that holds them back.

Karen Martin (ksmartin.com) is the founder of Karen Martin & Associates and the author of The Outstanding Organization.

INTELLIGENT ELIMINATION

Robert Morris

Many years ago during an interview, Katherine Hepburn was asked the secret to the success of her career. "Elimination! I have eliminated everyone and everything from my life that interferes with what I want to do and how I want to do it. Even Luddie, my former husband and dearest friend still. He simply had to go!"

Years later, I came upon Albert Einstein's observation: "Make everything as simple as possible, but not simpler." Then there was an observation by Peter Drucker: "There is surely nothing quite so useless as doing with great efficiency what should not be done at all." Still another by Michael Porter: "The essence of strategy is choosing what not to do."

These and other insights help explain why elimination can have great power if—huge "if"—it is combined with sound judgment and sufficient information.

One of my favorite anecdotes from the art world involves a French Romantic poet—I think it was Baudelaire, but I'm not certain—who was asked, "How to write a poem?" After a lengthy pause for reflection, he replied, "First draw a birdcage and leave the door open. Then wait and wait and wait. Eventually, maybe, a bird will fly in. Then erase the cage."

About 20 years ago, a severe frost was predicted here in Dallas. My wife said we had to trim back all the crepe myrtles or they would die. We cut them back almost to ground level. I feared that we had decapitated them. On the contrary, they were among the few smaller trees and bushes in our neighborhood that survived several days of subfreezing temperatures.

Years ago before my family and I moved from Connecticut to Rhode Island, a grizzled New Englander from United Van Lines came by the house to estimate the costs of packing and shipping our belongings. Then he met with us to discuss the situation. "With all due respect, ma'am, please remember that crap here will be crap there."

I think it's important to keep in mind that the power of elimination can have both positive and negative impact. Again, I stress the importance of sound judgment in combination with sufficient information.

As Jason Jennings suggests, "If it's DOA, bury it." Fair enough. But to invoke a gardening metaphor, I suggest that we also be careful not to rip out seedlings just to see how well they are growing.

Robert Morris (http://bobmorris.biz) specializes in accelerated executive development and high-impact organization change and is also an Amazon top 50 reviewer.

A TOTAL LIFE LIST

Bruce Rosenstein

The late Peter Drucker taught me something so valuable that I adapted it to help me organize my life. Drucker called it abandonment. It was a way to eliminate anything that was no longer at peak productivity. The idea is to regularly and ruthlessly put every activity and process on trial for its life to identify which ones still make sense and which should be dropped or scaled back.

I call it the total life list. Drucker led a busy life as a writer, consultant, and professor. I was lucky enough to spend time with him before his passing in 2005 while I was working for *USA Today* and later when writing a book. There were two striking instances when he stopped doing things he enjoyed because they either weren't working well (writing two novels) or were taking time away from more pressing work. One was writing novels, the other teaching Japanese art at Pomona College in southern California.

In one of my interviews with Drucker, he told me that in his experience, the people who were most satisfied and content with life "lived in more than one world," which ultimately gave me the title for the book. It also caused me to respond to him that what really matters is one's total life, the sum of all our activities inside and outside the workplace, as well as our interactions with the people in those various dimensions.

Afterward, I concluded that the only way to really know where one stood within these dimensions was to create a list that included just about everyone one knew and the activities in which one was involved. I came up with about a dozen different categories. It allowed me to see which activities in my life had outlived their usefulness or that I had outgrown and no longer enjoyed.

This list has had a profound effect on me. I can't think of anyone who couldn't profit from an honest, thorough listing of what he or she does in life and whom he or she does it with. If you're unsure of what you should stop doing, it helps to make sure that you know in detail exactly what you are doing now.

Bruce Rosenstein (brucerosenstein.com) is the managing editor of Leader to Leader, *a former business journalist for* USA Today, *and the author of* Living in More Than One World.

HALF TO WHOLE

Dan Keldsen

The year 2011 saw the single biggest change for me. It was a year of subtracting fear and routines that I hadn't fully realized I'd allowed to creep in and rule the way I was thinking, working, and living.

I had become an accidental solopreneur in late 2010 when my business partner of three years left to take a dream job. Suddenly I was forced to radically rethink what I was doing with myself. I walked into the office and thought, "Okay, so what does this business mean to me now that I'm literally the business now?"

As immediately paralyzing and confusing as it felt in the moment, suddenly being the last man standing was probably the best thing to ever happen to me. The "breaking" of the business as it went from two guys to one was most definitely the breakthrough I'd needed to take myself to the next level professionally and personally.

I've become far more focused on being myself than on being what I've allowed myself to become. I've eliminated nonproductive habits and instead operate in ways I've always believed to be more authentic. I've been rehumanizing myself into the strengths I can now look back and see were evident even in grade school (and which many teachers attempted to teach out of me), subtracting away the "corporate wisdom" that most of us have had the misfortune to be steeped in.

I wouldn't have ever thought to shrink the business by half. That decision wasn't mine to make, and I wouldn't have had the guts to leave to strike out on my own. But that breakthrough and shock really was a reset for me. I'm now seeing opportunities that I previously would have closed off as being distracting, inappropriate, or not interesting to my business partner.

It's not a huge surprise, then, that I've turned my rehumanizing insight into my single biggest focus moving forward, which is in understanding and applying insights into individual and group behavior. If nothing else, we're all human, and until we have a solid foundation for understanding and dealing with our fellow humans, everything else we do is likely to fail sooner or later. Think Humanity 2.0 before thinking Web or Enterprise 2.0, and the outcomes are dramatically different.

There's such a massive disconnect between what corporations believe will motivate people and how we actually think and act. I firmly believe we're just now seeing a massive subtraction of a whole world of assumptions about how companies should be owned and operated, and I'm excited to be in the middle of it, working as a change agent to help others get back to being human.

Dan Keldsen is the president of Information Architected (informationarchitected.com) and co-founder of Level 50 Software.

A SIMPLER WAY

Jamie Flinchbaugh

I spend much of my professional life helping people think in simpler terms, getting to the core of a problem or an idea to fit it on one page, to make the point in one story. However, it doesn't come naturally for me; it's a skill I've learned over time.

Part of my childhood was spent literally on the factory floor at Weldon Machine Tool, where we made cylindrical grinders. I've done my time doing tasks such as shoveling metal chips from the lathes to the scrap bin. But I also had the chance to do some more value-adding work as well. An early opportunity helped shape some of my thinking regarding simplicity in developing solutions.

We were building a grinder for a client. It was to include some software, which I would write, that would help generate the machine code. I was a college freshman, not an experienced programmer. And I was programming on a computer with low processing power: my first runs of the program took well over 12 hours.

After my first trials with a working program, we sent the code back to the client, only to hear that it was wrong. I was not in a position to disagree, because my engineering experience was limited and, of course, they were the client. I kept digging and digging and couldn't figure out what I had done wrong.

A week or so later the client called back and said, "Sorry, but your code is right. We thought it was wrong because it doesn't match ours, but your approach is actually more accurate than ours."

Here's what happened. The old process involved someone sending the part drawings to an engineer. Those drawings would sit on the engineer's desk, waiting, usually for something like six weeks. The engineer would then develop the machine code after doing some calculations based on the drawing.

I went a simpler way. I bypassed engineering and took numbers straight from the drawing and used them to generate the part profile and code. The end result was that instead of sitting on an engineer's desk for six weeks, a machine operator could enter some numbers directly from the drawing and generate the code in six minutes. That turned out to be pretty useful.

Just because something was always done that way, that doesn't mean that it is right or best. Sometimes a fresh and direct look at how to do something will yield the simplest and best path forward.

Jamie Flinchbaugh (leanlearningcenter.com) is a cofounder of the Lean Learning Center and the co-author of The Hitchhiker's Guide to Lean: Lessons from the Road.

PASS IT ON

Brian Buck

 Early in my career I learned a powerful lesson: showing others how to do what I do best frees me to grow and learn something else while benefiting the other person at the same time.

The power of this was driven home to me years ago. I had created an Excel macro that helped reduce tedious steps for processing claims. I became so married to that macro that my professional growth slowed down, because all my time was spent preserving it.

But I missed the creativity of doing something new.

I showed my coworkers how to make changes to the program when they wanted to update it. A few of them really loved learning a new skill. In the end, what made it work was that I was able to transfer ownership to them. I was free to be assigned to a new project and begin growing again.

I repeated this pattern throughout my career: learn something new, become proficient at it, pass the knowledge and responsibility to someone else, and then use the freed time to gain new or deeper knowledge about a topic.

Breaking free from having to be the sole source of knowledge or skill by sharing it with others has given me the opportunity for many professional breakthroughs. More important, I have been able to help others learn things that make their jobs easier.

Knowledge is not power. Shared knowledge is power. If you create new knowledge, don't hoard it; set it—and yourself—free.

Pass it on.

Brian Buck coaches organizational teams to remove waste through kaizen *and blogs at improve withme.com.*

LAW NO. 6

DOING SOMETHING *ISN'T*

ALWAYS BETTER THAN

DOING NOTHING

*All men's miseries derive from the inability
to sit still in a quiet room alone.*
Blaise Pascal

Boyd Matson looks every bit the adventure journalist he is: rugged, sturdy, and built for danger. His *National Geographic* television series *Wild Chronicles* and *Explorer* and weekly column "Unbound" seem to say it all: he was born to be wild, live on the edge, climb every mountain, dance with death, and test every limit imaginable. He's been scratched, bitten, chased, attacked, pooped on, and even kissed by animals ordinary folks see only in the zoo.

Boyd taught me an extremely valuable, in fact lifesaving, lesson: how to stand still when the hippos charge.* That strategy underscores the sixth and final law of subtraction: *Doing something* isn't *always better than doing nothing.*

Doing nothing is, of course, impossible. One of my favorite exercises in my creativity workshops is to begin with five minutes of doing nothing. No one can do it, because it can't be done. Even the meditators are doing *something.*

When we say we are doing nothing, what we really mean is that we are taking a break from our normal business in some way. And as it turns out, that is when our brains are the most creative.

How and why that's true is the subject of this final chapter.

DAYDREAM BELIEVIN'

In late spring 1905, an utterly frustrated 26-year-old Albert Einstein decided to pour his head out to his friend and fellow Swiss patent office worker Michele Besso. Einstein revealed the puzzle he had wrestled with for the last seven years: either James Maxwell's equation or Isaac Newton's laws had to be wrong, but he couldn't figure out which one. Both were pillars of modern physics, but they were completely incompatible. The solution would unify all of physics.

---

* We both spoke at Southern Nazarene University's Zig Ziglar Center for Ethical Leadership in 2007. I followed up with him in 2008, learning more about his talk "How to Stand Still When the Hippos Charge" because it was one of the most elegant solutions I'd ever heard.

Einstein laid out the issue to Michele: the intricacies of Maxwell's theory about light traveling at a constant speed contradicting Newton's concept of absolute space and time. He talked for hours until he once again surrendered to the problem—completely exhausted both mentally and physically—whereupon he announced his defeat and intention to abandon the quest for a solution. Ten years was more than enough time to devote it.

Melancholy from his failure, Einstein pushed his thoughts to the back of his mind and headed home. Riding in a streetcar, he gazed out at the famous clock tower that dominated the city of Bern. Suppose, he pondered, his streetcar raced away from the clock tower at the speed of light. What would happen? He was suddenly struck with the realization that since light could not catch up to the streetcar, the clock would appear stopped, but his own clock—say, his pocket watch—in the streetcar would beat normally.

"A storm broke loose in my mind," Einstein recalled later. "Suddenly I understood where the key to the problem lay." Here's what Einstein recorded on a discograph in 1924, nearly 20 years after changing the world with his theory of special relativity:

> After seven years of reflection in vain, the solution came to me suddenly with the thought that our concepts and laws of space and time can only claim validity insofar as they stand in a clear relation to our experiences; and that experience could very well lead to the alteration of these concepts and laws. By a revision of the concept of simultaneity into a more malleable form, I thus arrived at the special theory of relativity.

The circumstances surrounding Einstein's revelation reveal another dimension to the notion of a break being the important part of a breakthrough. Making a break is one dimension, as we saw in Chapter 5. Taking a break—a time-out from the problem at hand—is the other dimension.

Einstein's sudden insight is not the exception to the rule. Take a look at the following handful of stories by noteworthy individuals talking about the moment of their respective breakthroughs. As you read the memoirs, ask yourself what they all have in common.

Here is chemist Friedrich August Kekulé von Stradonitz on discovering the shape of the benzene ring in the mid-1800s:

I fell into a reverie, and lo, the atoms were gambolling before my eyes. I was sitting writing on my textbook, but the work did not progress; my thoughts were elsewhere. I turned my chair to the fire and dozed. Again the atoms were gambolling before my eyes. This time the smaller groups kept modestly in the background. My mental eye, rendered more acute by repeated visions of the kind, could now distinguish larger structures of manifold conformation: long rows sometimes more closely fitted together all twining and twisting in snake-like motion. But look! What was that? One of the snakes had seized hold of its own tail, and the form whirled mockingly before my eyes. As if by a flash of lightning I awoke; and this time I spent the rest of the night working out the consequences of the hypothesis.

Here is physicist Richard Feynman on coming up with a Nobel Prize–winning idea for quantum electrodynamics in 1946:

I was in the cafeteria and some guy, fooling around, throws a plate in the air. As the plate went up in the air I saw it wobble, and I noticed the red medallion of Cornell on the plate going around. It was pretty obvious to me that the medallion went around faster than the wobbling. I had nothing to do, so I started to figure out the motion of the revolving plate. I went on to work out equations of wobbles. And before I knew it (it was a very short time) I was playing—working, really—with the same old problem that I loved so much, that I had stopped working on when I went to Los Alamos: my thesis-type problems; all those old-fashioned, wonderful things. It was effortless. It was easy to play with these things. It was like uncorking a bottle: Everything flowed out effortlessly. I almost tried to resist it! There was no importance to what I was doing, but ultimately there was. The diagrams and the whole business that I got the Nobel Prize for came from that piddling around with the wobbling plate.

Here is theoretical physicist and mathematician Freeman Dyson on his seminal 1948 paper reconciling the conflicting theories of Richard Feynman and Julian Schwinger:

I got onto a Greyhound bus and traveled nonstop for three days and nights as far as Chicago. This time I had nobody to talk to. The roads were too bumpy for me to read, and so I sat and looked out of the window and gradually fell into a comfortable stupor. As we were droning across Nebraska on the third day, something suddenly happened. For two weeks I had not thought about physics, and now it came bursting into my consciousness like an explosion. Feynman's pictures and Schwinger's equations began sorting themselves out in my head with a clarity they had never had before. For the first time I was able to put them all together. For an hour or two I arranged and rearranged the pieces. Then I knew how it all fitted. I had no pencil or paper, but everything was so clear I did not need to write it down. During the rest of the day as we watched the sun go down over the prairie, I was mapping out in my head the shape of the paper I would write when I got to Princeton.

Here is legendary designer Milton Glaser on coming up with the iconic "I ♥ NY" logo in 1977:

> I send in my proposal [to the New York State Department of Commerce] and it's approved. Everybody likes it. And if I were a normal person, I'd stop thinking about the project. But I can't. Something about it just doesn't feel right. I can't get the damn problem out of my head. And then, about a week after the first concept was approved, I'm sitting in a cab, stuck in traffic. I often carry spare pieces of paper in my pocket, and so I get the paper out and I start to draw. And I'm thinking and drawing and then I get it. I see the whole design in my head. I see the typewriter typeface and the big round red heart smack-dab in the middle. I know that this is how it should go. Design is the conscious imposition of meaningful order. That sounds grandiose, but it's just the process of taking an idea that isn't clear and making it a little more clear. I could tell you a bullshit story about what exactly led to the idea, but the truth is that I don't know. Maybe I saw a red heart out of the corner of my eye? Maybe I heard the word? But that's the way it always works. You keep on trying to fix it, to make the design a little

bit more interesting, a little bit better. And then, if you're really stubborn and persistent and lucky, you eventually get there.

Here is author J. K. Rowling on the idea for *Harry Potter*:

In 1990, my then boyfriend and I decided to move up to Manchester together. It was after a weekend's flat-hunting, when I was travelling back to London on my own on a crowded train, that the idea for Harry Potter simply fell into my head. I had been writing almost continuously since the age of six but I had never been so excited about an idea before. To my immense frustration, I didn't have a functioning pen with me, and I was too shy to ask anybody if I could borrow one. I think, now, that this was probably a good thing, because I simply sat and thought, for four (delayed train) hours, and all the details bubbled up in my brain, and this scrawny, black-haired, bespectacled boy who didn't know he was a wizard became more and more real to me. I think that perhaps if I had had to slow down the ideas so that I could capture them on paper I might have stifled some of them (although sometimes I do wonder, idly, how much of what I imagined on that journey I had forgotten by the time I actually got my hands on a pen). I began to write "*Philosopher's Stone*" that very evening.

In the fall of 2007 I was invited to the headquarters of 3M, which is just a few miles from downtown St. Paul, Minnesota, to speak to several different audiences about Toyota's approach to innovation, learn about 3M's approach to innovation, and tour the campus. 3M is one of the most innovative companies in the world, with as many products as employees, and has been for over 75 years. My sponsors gave me a wonderful book on the history of innovation at 3M, and upon arrival back at my home, I had two large boxes waiting for me, chock full of samples from the 3M product family: tapes, glues, cleaners, fasteners, sealants, and every size of Post-its I could hope to need. I still haven't used them all.

Like most people, I knew the famous 3M story of Post-it Notes. Arthur Fry, the 3M engineer responsible for developing it, recalls his 1974 breakthrough this way in a 1990 radio interview:

It came one Sunday morning. I was singing in the church choir. I would get upset when pieces of paper that I would use as a bookmark would fall out of my music. I thought there must be a better way of making a bookmark. It was during a dull sermon, and my mind was wandering. I thought about a friend of mine [Spencer Silver] in our central research who had developed an adhesive. I went back to the laboratory the next morning and made samples of a bookmark. And then later on, in using one of these bookmarks as a note to my boss, he wrote the answer on it and stuck it on something he used to send it back me. During a coffee break we thought, "Aha! We don't have just a bookmark, what we have is a whole systems approach!"

Although 3M is in the adhesive business—and has been since the early 1930s when researcher Richard Drew slapped some adhesive on the back of some DuPont cellophane to produce what we now call Scotch Tape—Arthur was *not* trying to invent the thing he invented. He, like Einstein and the others, was simply daydreaming.

Wandering Minds

What all these sudden insights have in common is that they came at strange times and places: in a streetcar, on a train or bus, while driving a car. They happened after an intense, prolonged struggle with a particular problem, followed by taking a break. They involved a change of scene and time away from the problem-solving activity.

Each involved a wandering mind, a distracted mind, a daydreaming mind—in reality, a calm and relaxed mind—a mind that those involved would say was doing nothing. That, of course, is not the case. As we now know and as was conclusively shown in 2009, it's when we are engaged in a calming activity rather than wracking our brains over the problem at hand—exercising, driving, meditating, hiking, showering, dozing—that our brains do their best work. It's when we're not *trying* to think creatively that we're often the most creative. That's when a still mysterious process in the right hemisphere of the brain makes connections between seemingly unrelated things, and those connections then bubble up as sudden insights, as if out of nowhere.

Neuroscientists are learning more and more about the creative power of the wandering mind, experimenting with various states of relaxation, and studying the production of sudden insights while tracking brain activity with functional magnetic resonance imaging (fMRI) and electroencephalography (EEG).

Several articles appearing in publications such as *Scientific Mind* helped me sort out and make sense out of the latest discoveries and what the results might imply for people wishing to tap into their natural creativity.

One science journalist concluded that Arthur Fry's daydreaming was integral to his idea for Post-it Notes. The boring sermon set the stage for a daydream by allowing Fry to tune out and divert his attention elsewhere. It was Fry's wandering mind that enabled him to make the connection between the problem of his makeshift bookmarks falling out of the hymnal and his colleague's not-so-sticky adhesive.

The kind of thinking that enables these unexpected connections is thought to be the stuff of creativity, and people who daydream seem to be better at it than those who don't or can't. The trick, though, seems to be daydreaming and letting your mind wander yet remaining just aware enough to recognize a sudden insight when it comes. After all, what good is daydreaming if you don't notice your aha moment when it hits? What researchers make clear is that it isn't enough just to be a prolific daydreamer—it's the ability to let your mind wander in such a way that you pay just enough attention to the problem at hand, but can still sense that instant when your daydreaming produces an insightful solution.

This more than anything is the fundamental characteristic of all those brilliant flashes of genius, from Einstein to Rowling to Fry. Yes, they were all daydreaming. But all noticed the connection when it appeared.

What that means is that not all daydreaming is created equal. Sitting around the house all day in one long protracted daydream won't produce any insights unless there was a certain density of attention paid to a specific problem that preceded it. It's *dedicated* daydreaming—purposeful mind wandering—that yields productive creativity.

In other words, there's science and art to daydreaming. Science first.

The science of daydreaming is not exactly new. In fact, it's been 20 years since Washington University neurologist Marcus Raichle noticed something strange and surprising during a study of visual perception using an fMRI scanner: the brain activity of the participants during the breaks between tasks was extraordinarily high, just the opposite of what you'd assume would be the case for a brain at rest. And it wasn't just worthless noise; it was the brain's creativity center in the frontal cortex that was all lit up. As Raichle tells it: "When you don't use a muscle, that muscle isn't doing much. But when your brain is supposedly doing nothing, it's really doing a tremendous amount."

Within a few years after his discovery, Raichle was able to determine why our brains get so busy when we're absentmindedly doing nothing: it's our default mental state. In other words, a wandering mind may be something hardwired into our mental machinery. It turns out that our default state is most engaged when we're doing something that doesn't require much conscious attention: driving, staring off into space, daydreaming. What Raichle's fMRI studies showed conclusively was that during the absentminded default state previously assumed to be one of mental dormancy, the brain is in fact at its most creative.

In his 2011 book *Thinking, Fast and Slow,* psychologist Daniel Kahneman labels our default mental state as "System 1." System 1 is a quick, reflexive, effortless, unconscious, and intuitive network. In fact, Raichle termed it the "default network." Kahneman says that System 2 is a slow, labored, effortful, conscious, and analytic network. System 1 handles the routine tasks that don't require much attention, while System 2 handles higher-level, complex problem solving. Most researchers refer to Kahneman's System 2 as our executive network.

Until just recently, though, researchers thought that the two operated on an either-or basis; the brain's default network was the only part of the brain thought to be active when our minds wander. But a new study published in the *Proceedings of the National Academy of Sciences* by cognitive neuroscientist Kalina Christoff sheds new and profound light on the subject. Dr. Christoff placed subjects inside an fMRI scanner, where they performed the mindless task of repeatedly pushing a button. In other words, she activated the default network by letting boredom produce wandering minds. She then tracked performance on the task as well as moment-to-moment attentiveness. The default network's activity was high, as expected. The surprise, though, was that the brain fMRI scans also showed high executive network activity. *The whole brain was engaged.*

"This is a surprising finding, that these two brain networks are activated in parallel," says Dr. Christoff. "People assumed that when your mind wandered, it was empty. But this study shows our brains are very active when we daydream. Mind wandering is a much more active state than we ever imagined, much more active than during reasoning with a complex problem. When you daydream, you may not be achieving your immediate goal—say, reading a book or paying attention in class—but your mind may be taking that time to address more important questions in your life."

The idea that people struggling to solve complicated problems might be better off switching to a simpler task and letting their mind wander is a monumentally important one; by most estimates we spend a third of our waking lives daydreaming.

"You can see regions of these networks becoming active just prior to people arriving at an insight," Dr. Christoff says. The implication is that an unfocused mind may make surprising connections more effectively than does a mind engaged in methodical reasoning and thus create the mental framework for new and creative ideas. But it's not just that when the mind wanders in a daydream that the two networks work in unison. It's that it may be the *only* time.

So what is it about a purposefully daydreaming, dedicated wandering mind that is different from an intensely focused analytic mind?

Surfing the Alpha Waves

For over 30 years, researchers have linked creativity with low-frequency brain waves known as alpha waves. Alpha waves are slow waves, under 12 hertz (Hz), and indicate a relaxed but aware brain. They are the brain waves of a daydreaming, wandering mind.

Colin Martindale of the University of Maine used a series of electro-encephalographic studies in the late 1970s to show that highly creative people exhibit more alpha wave activity during creative tasks than do less creative people. Martindale suggested that higher alpha wave activity indicated defocused attention and less inhibition, meaning that creative people were allowing more unedited information into their conscious awareness during creative work. A research team led by Andreas Fink at the University of Graz in Austria recently replicated Martindale's findings but has a different interpretation: the increased alpha wave activity indicates that the brain is focusing internally rather than on the outside world.

In 2009, I briefly introduced readers of *In Pursuit of Elegance* to the work of Mark Beeman, a cognitive neuroscientist at Northwestern University who had demonstrated by using fMRI the actual brain wave differences in the two different networks. Volunteers who had a moment of sudden insight when solving a series of anagrams showed a burst of fast brain waves of over 40 Hz—known as gamma waves—right around the aha moment. Preceding the gamma waves, however, was a resting state of slower alpha waves. Beeman's conclusion was that it's a quiet mind that sets the stage and gives rise to breakthrough moments. But the data from fMRI weren't as clean as he wanted.

More recently, Beeman teamed with psychologist John Kounios of Drexel University to publish a study in which they pinpointed the precise moment of the gamma burst. They used both fMRI and the faster EEG to scan brain patterns of subjects engaged in solving word-association problems. (For example: What word can form a compound word with all three of the following words: *crab, pine, sauce?*)

Subjects signaled when they had the answer and whether they got the solution through methodical trial-and-error or it suddenly popped into their heads. As in previous studies, the sudden insighters all displayed prolonged alpha waves first, followed by a right hemisphere gamma wave burst three milliseconds—a lifetime in brain speed—before the aha moment. The insighters simply knew the answer and had no doubts about it. (The answer, by the way, is *apple.*)

Those who took the more analytic approach did not exhibit the same alpha wave prologue or the gamma wave burst and didn't experience the exhilarating revelation. Beeman and Kounios concluded that alpha activity focuses attention inward, whereas the gamma burst coincides with the sudden arrival of the solution in conscious awareness. The other interesting thing they found was that the gamma burst was usually preceded by a change in alpha wave intensity in the part of the brain that controls vision, evidence that right before a sudden insight, the brain was doing its own version of what we do when we want to concentrate: we close our eyes.

Psychologist Joydeep Bhattacharya of the University of London's Goldsmiths College published a study in the *Journal of Cognitive Neuroscience* showing alpha and gamma brain wave patterns that allowed him to identify whether a person would have a sudden insight up to eight seconds before it actually happened.

Bhattacharya's conclusion is the strongest: without sufficient alpha wave activity, there simply will be no aha moment.

That brings us to the art of purposeful daydreaming: how do we go about producing higher levels of alpha waves? There are several ways, and what follows will conclude our tour of the laws of subtraction.

DOING NOTHING

Is it really possible to get better results at work by doing nothing?

According to a 2009 survey of over 600 workers in the United States by the Society for Human Resource Management, 70 percent of employees work beyond the scheduled time—staying late, taking work home, and working on weekends.

Harvard Business School researchers Leslie Perlow and Jessica Porter surveyed 1,000 people in professional service firms and found that nearly half worked over 65 hours per week, not including nearly 25 hours spent connecting with their work while outside the office.

"They believe an 'always on' ethic is essential if they and their firms are to succeed in the global marketplace," wrote Perlow and Porter in their four-year study, which was published in *Harvard Business Review*.

Their research seems to confirm just the opposite, that not working can yield better work. In the experiment, members of a dozen consulting teams at Boston Consulting Group (BCG) were required to take "predictable time off" every week, defined as one uninterrupted evening free each week after 6 p.m.: no work contact whatsoever and no BlackBerrys.

The downtime was awkward for many and nerve-racking for some, and a few fought the idea, fearful of poor performance ratings or more weekend work. The goal was to teach people that one can tune out completely for a time and still produce great work.

It worked. BCG internal surveys showed that within six months, consultants were more satisfied with their jobs and work-life balance and more likely to stay with the firm compared with those who weren't part of the study. BCG clients told Perlow and Porter that the teams turned out better work in part as a result of "more open dialogue among team members" and that "the improved communication also sparked new processes that enhanced the teams' ability to work most efficiently and effectively."

It worked so well that BCG made it a policy.

TUNE OUT TO ZONE IN

Chapter 5 introduced the Zen principle of *datsuzoku*, which refers to a break with convention and routine. The Zen aesthetic principle of *seijaku* (say-JAH-koo) deals with the content of *datsuzoku*. To a Zen practitioner, it is in states of active calm, tranquillity, solitude, and quietude that we find the essence of creative energy. It seems the Zen masters got there long before neuroscientists did. Perhaps that's why Buddhist "adepts"— those with over 10,000 hours of mindful meditation to their name—are one of the most studied groups: they exhibit abnormally high levels of alpha waves.

What's interesting about all the cognitive neuroscientific findings is the central paradox at play. The actual right brain process responsible for our aha moments remains unknown. All we know is that we cannot speed up the sudden insight-manufacturing process or somehow push it to work harder or more intensely. We can only let go, tune out as it were, and find that Zen place where the alpha waves flow. We need to take a break, relax, stop thinking, and do nothing while remaining aware that we are doing so. We need to learn how to *purposefully* do nothing.

There is another aspect to the paradox. It's not just that we need to be in a relaxed and unfocused state of mind in order to let the brain make its creative connections at its own pace. It's that if we don't or can't release our focus, if we insist on maintaining an analytical stranglehold on the problem, if we can't redirect our attention from an outward direction to a more inward one, we may actually block those creative connections from ever being made. At the very least, we will inhibit our ability to recognize an insight once a connection is made.

In other words, not only is doing something not always better than doing nothing, it can make matters worse. The irony is that trying to be creative might only make us less so. The implication is significant, because it reverses ages of organizational thinking that assumes the best way to achieve a creative breakthrough is to lock ourselves in a room for hours at a time and brainstorm over the details of the problem we're trying to solve. Focusing intently that way inadvertently denies the brain the break it needs to manufacture creative insights.

And therein lies the catch. As the consultants in the Boston Consulting Group time-out experiment revealed, we're reluctant to take those breaks. Certainly we don't include them or build them in as a formal part of our problem-solving efforts. Yes, many companies now follow the policy that 3M originated (yes, 3M, not Google) and institutionalized of encouraging people to devote 15 to 20 percent of their time to working on new ideas that interest them. But that is *datsuzoku*, not *seijaku*. Arthur Fry's sudden insight about sticky notes did not occur during that time, although he did use that time in the ensuing months to develop the idea fully.

There are at least two reasons we don't take time out more often. The first is fear. Stepping away from our work is counterintuitive. It somehow feels wrong, like preemptive surrender. It's scary to ease up, because we think that we may lose our momentum and that if we take our eye off the problem even for a second, we may lose the energy we've invested. But the result is that we get anxious when the solution to whatever we're struggling with remains elusive, and it's easy to start doubting our creativity, our abilities, and even our intelligence: "I'm obviously stupid because I can't figure this out."

That's the cue to take a break, but we still don't because of the second reason: we don't know how. We haven't practiced enough to develop a reliable and comfortable way to productively tune out and quiet our minds.

That's the art of *seijaku*, and there are a variety of ways to do it.

1. Mindful Meditation

Executives at GE, 3M, Bloomberg, Green Mountain Coffee, and Salesforce .com do it. Google teaches a course in it at Google University. Ford chairman William Ford does it, as do former corporate chiefs Bill George of Medtronic and Bob Shapiro of Monsanto. Phil Jackson and Tiger Woods do it. Oracle chief Larry Ellison does it and asks his executives to do it several times a day. Chip Conley, founder of Joie de Vivre hotels and author of *Emotional Equations,* does it. Thomas Edison did it. The "it" is mindful meditation.

According to Bill George, now a Harvard leadership professor and bestselling author, meditation has been an integral part of his career. He meditates twice a day and during his tenure as Medtronic's CEO designated one of the company's conference rooms for mental breaks, encouraging employees to give meditation a try. Google in 2007 initiated a mindfulness and meditation course at Google University, encouraging employees to use the practice to increase self-awareness, focus, and attention.

New research from the UCLA Laboratory of Neuro Imaging suggests that people who meditate show more gray matter in certain regions of the brain, show stronger connections between brain regions, and show less age-related brain atrophy. In other words, meditation may make your brain bigger, faster, and younger.

The researchers used a type of brain imaging known as diffusion tensor imaging (DTI), a relatively new imaging mode that provides insights into the structural connectivity of the brain. According to lead researcher Eileen Luders, herself a meditator, "Meditation appears to be a powerful mental exercise with the potential to change the physical structure of the brain at large. Meditation might not only cause changes in brain anatomy by inducing growth but also by preventing reduction."

If you want to get started with meditation, read the contribution by Dr. Jeffrey Schwartz at the end of the chapter.

2. Neurofeedback

Not everyone can meditate. Neurofeedback training is another way to learn to quiet the mind. It worked for Italy's 2006 World Cup championship team, notorious for its constant presence in the secret mind room.

Neurofeedback training uses EEG. EEG works by detecting electrical signals given by brain waves, all of which have different wavelengths and frequencies. Neurofeedback works the way almost any feedback mechanism works, whether a mirror, a videotape of your performance, or even a live audience: your actions get fed back to you so that you can adjust accordingly. In this case, you can see and hear in real time what's going on between your mind and your brain through the images on the computer screen and the music that's being played, all of which corresponds to the various types of brain waves you're generating. Your brain then learns to improve the management of these states. Once these new developmental skills are learned, they eventually become automatic, like riding a bike or trying out shoes—no thinking required.

The underlying philosophy is the same as that behind mindful meditation—indirectly influencing the physical connections in the brain by directing the mind—but using a bit of technology as a guide. Here, by training your brain to a resting state, you not only set yourself up to more automatically find the zone but also set the stage for the kind of creative insights that result in an aha moment.

3. Pulsing

Pulsing is the simplest and easiest and most immediate way to build breaks into your day: work in 90-minute cycles separated by short breaks. Go for a walk, change the scene, exercise, doodle, listen to music that relaxes you, shower (if that's an option)—anything that has a renewal effect on you and gives you the feeling of a second wind, even if you think you don't need it. You do.

The late physiologist Nathaniel Kleitman, who discovered rapid eye movement (REM) sleep and correlated it with dreaming and brain activity, showed that we move through five stages of light to deep sleep in recurring 90-minute periods. These are "ultradian" cycles, and they have a parallel in our waking life: when we're awake, we move from higher to lower alertness every 90 minutes. After working at high intensity for more than 90 minutes, our brains begin to shut down. We become more reactive and less capable of thinking clearly and reflectively or seeing the big picture.

And here's the thing: our bodies clearly signal that rhythm in the form of restlessness, hunger, drowsiness, and loss of focus. Generally we either ignore or override those signals because we have a lot to do and many ways to artificially pump up our energy with various supplements. But that just defeats the purpose: mind quieting.

The psychologist K. Anders Ericsson, known for his research and theories on expertise, points out that top performers in fields ranging from music to science to sports tend to work in approximately 90-minute cycles and then take a break.

We are designed to pulse, to move between spending and renewing energy. Taking time to renew every 90 minutes keeps the body in alignment with its natural rhythms.

4. Retreat

Sometimes the antidote to a chatterbox brain is a short retreat from the workaday world, combining *datsuzoku* and *seijaku*.

Since the *Wall Street Journal* revealed it in 2005, Bill Gates's "Think Week"—the twice-yearly solitary sabbatical at a secret hideaway taken by the Microsoft chairman—has become legendary. Bill takes a helicopter or seaplane to a tiny but tidy two-story, one-bedroom clapboard cottage on a quiet waterfront somewhere in the Pacific Northwest. No visitors are allowed, including friends, family, and colleagues. The only outsider he sees is the caretaker, who brings him two simple meals each day.

"He starts the morning in bed poring through papers mostly by Microsoft engineers, executives, and product managers and scribbling notes on the covers," writes *WSJ* reporter Robert Guth, the first and only journalist ever allowed into the secret location. "Skipping breakfast, he patters upstairs in his stocking feet to read more papers. Noon and dinnertime bring him back downstairs to read papers over meals at the kitchen table, where he has a view of the Olympic Mountains. His main staple for the week is a steady stream of Diet Orange Crush." The setting is quiet and peaceful and allows Gates to relax and unwind, all the while filling his mind with information and ideas.

Writer Caitlin Kelly found new insights into her life and relationship by going on an eight-day silent Buddhist retreat with her husband, Jose, a devout follower of Dzogchen, an esoteric and austere form of Tibetan Buddhism. Held at a former Catholic monastery high on the eastern shore of the Hudson River and overlooking West Point, it was his birthday gift to her—a strange one at that, given that Caitlin is as religious as Jose is, but of the Episcopalian persuasion. Each day was devoted to attaining *rigpa*—awareness—with the goal of silence being to shut out the world and enable a deeper resonance with the daily Buddhist teachings, meditations, and yoga. Additional prohibitions included technology of any kind.

"The point of the retreat was to break habits and examine the emotional and physical crutches we rely on," said Caitlin. "Such profound silence was at first shocking but soon became deeply soothing. The noises of normal life disappeared: ringing phones, someone's leaky earbuds, the clicking of computer keys, the screech of bus brakes. I wasn't obsessed with toxic minutiae of the news or mindless television. Hours consumed by Facebook were replaced by lectures on how to sharpen one's sense of awareness. Surprisingly, I loved it. As the retreat ended, I felt regret. I loved our temporary reprieve from the social reflexes of everyday life. But I really felt the retreat's effects in the weeks afterward. . . . We experienced an earthquake and a hurricane, which normally would have sent me over the edge. But now, when I'm stressed, I take several long, deep, slow breaths. And it works."

5. Travel

Cognitive research shows that familiarity can stifle creativity, and it is when we distance ourselves from our most pressing problems and our usual stomping grounds that the imagination fires up. One way to achieve that distance is to travel for extended periods.

A 2009 study published by the American Psychological Association demonstrated that the longer MBA students at the Kellogg School of Management had spent living abroad, the more likely they were to solve the famous 1945 Duncker candle problem, considered to be a measure of creative insight.

According to the study, the kind of creative problem solving required for adapting to another culture and generating a new social identity produces new neural connections in the brain, yielding new psychological associations.

6. Long Walks

Long walks and hikes are the preferred method of psychologist Jonathan Schooler, who runs the META Lab at the University of California, Santa

Barbara (UCSB), and who helped pioneer the study of daydreaming and the wandering mind. Schooler takes a dedicated daydreaming walk every day on the beautiful bluffs above the Pacific Ocean, just north of Santa Barbara, and says he always knows when he desperately needs a daydreaming walk: when the problem seems impossible to solve, when there's no feeling of knowing, and no sense of progress.

A recent study confirms that walking promotes the connections we call creativity: our two brain networks working in tandem to produce new insights. The study was led by University of Illinois psychologist Art Kramer and followed 65 adults who joined a walking group or a stretching and toning group for a year. All the participants were sedentary before the study, reporting less than two episodes of physical activity lasting 30 minutes or more in the previous six months. Rather than focusing on specific brain structures, the study looked at the brain activity occurring in the default and executive networks. The researchers measured the participants' brain connectivity and performance on cognitive tasks at the beginning of the study, six months later, and after a year of either walking or toning and stretching.

At the end of the year, connectivity in the default network—which you'll recall dominates our daydreaming mode—was significantly improved in the brains of the walkers but not in the stretching and toning group's brains. The walkers also had increased connectivity in the executive network, which you'll recall handles complex analytic work, performing significantly better on cognitive tests.

7. Napping

At the University of Lübeck in Germany, neuroendocrinologist Ullrich Wagner has demonstrated that the ultimate break—sleep—increases the likelihood of creative insights. In one experiment, he gave volunteers some Mensa-style number sequences to solve, along with two logical rules to use in manipulating them to find the pattern. But there was a single, simpler "hidden" rule that they might discover as they worked through the sequences. The subjects were allowed to practice several times with the rules and then told to take a break. Some took naps; some didn't. Upon returning to the experiment to continue doing problems, those who had taken a nap found the hidden rule much more often than did those who hadn't.

Wagner believes what all neuroscientists do: the quiet mind enables the brain to clear itself and in effect reboot, all the while forming new connections and associations.

8. Long, Languid Showers

This one needs no explanation, which is good, because I could find no research on the subject.

THE ULTIMATE SUBTRACTION

What happens if you don't or can't learn to let go, to calm and quiet your mind through a technique such as those just discussed? What if you aren't able to effectively do nothing when you really need to?

The scientific answer is that your executive network (Kahneman's System 2)—will take over. Your free-flowing default network (Kahneman's System 1) will take a back seat. What was easy and effortless will become forced and labored. Because your executive function is your impulse and inhibition control center, it can absolutely handcuff you if you can't quiet it on command.

In other words, you'll suffocate your creativity. You'll be so worried about making a mistake, you'll cease to perform. Jana Novotna should know. In 1993, she lost the Wimbledon women's final to Steffi Graf on the hundredth anniversary of that final in just this way.

It has gone down in sports history as "the Choke." On the muggy but breezy afternoon of July 4, 1993, Jana found herself five points from taking the crown from the reigning Wimbledon queen, Steffi, who had won four of the last five titles, including the two previous ones. Everything was going her way, and she could do no wrong, or so it seemed. And then she double-faulted, sending both serves into the net. She missed a fairly routine volley on the next exchange. At game point, she dumped an overhead smash into the net. Steffi took the next game easily, and Jana seemed rattled, so much so that she allowed Steffi to win the next game after being up by two points. She was still ahead, but everyone watching could see that her body language had changed from confident belief to head-hanging defeat. She was a completely different player from the one she had been just two games earlier.

What happened next stunned the crowd: Jana hit six straight service faults into the net. Everyone could see her talking to herself, shaking her head, berating herself. Her movements seemed stiff, off balance, and slow. Some remarked that she looked like an absolute beginner as she missed easy shot after easy shot, losing to Steffi 4–6.

It wasn't nerves. Jana was no rookie, having won the doubles title on two previous occasions: 1989 and 1990. She had upset Gabriela Sabatini and Martina Navratilova on the same court just days before.

As the duchess of Kent handed her the second place trophy at the awards ceremony, a visibly distraught Novotna burst into tears and cried on the shoulder of the duchess, who tried to comfort her.

The most telling comment was by Steffi Graf, who told journalists afterward, "It's a human brain and so difficult to train, you know, to prepare it."

Self-Subtraction

We each face our own charging hippo every bit as deadly as those Boyd Matson handles easily by doing nothing. It comes in a different form to each of us yet is marked by its excessive, confusing, wasteful, unnatural, hazardous, hard-to-use, or ugly features. It is ubiquitous, voracious, and relentless. Learning what it means to stand still in the face of it is no easy matter. But perhaps we make matters far worse than they need to be. Perhaps the way to win in this age of excess everything is simply to learn to get out of our own way.

That more than anything else may be the ultimate act of subtraction.

SILHOUETTES

IN SUBTRACTION

Jeffrey Schwartz

Bill Jensen

Tony Schwartz

David Sherwin

Jeff Unger

Kevin Meyer

Jonathan Kay

PleaseFindThis

STOP THINKING

Jeffrey Schwartz

I meditate daily for one hour without fail. I've been involved in mindful meditation for over 30 years. I recommend it highly. To get started, here are the original Buddhist instructions.

Sit still in a chair in a quiet room for 20 minutes and just watch yourself breathe. Pick a time and a place when you can be reasonably sure no one will interrupt you. Close the door to minimize outer distractions. Sit comfortably in a chair or cross-legged on the floor with your hands resting in your lap. You can close your eyes, or you can keep them open but unfocused. Place your attention on the inner rim of your nostrils, where you can feel the subtle movement of air as you breathe in and out.

Now "watch" your breathing go in, go out, go in, go out. Make a mental note for each in breath and out breath like this: "breathing in," breathing out." Or just "in" and "out." Try to be aware of the entire in breath from the time it starts to the time it stops. This is the time to make the mental note "breathing in," if that's your choice of terms. Don't worry about the exact words; it's the process of observing yourself that's critical. Then try to be aware of the entire out breath from the time it starts to the time it stops. This is the time to make the mental note "breathing out."

If you suddenly notice that your mind has wandered away from your breathing, just make a mental note of that, for example, "wandering, wandering," or "thinking, thinking," or "imagining, imagining." Then gently bring your attention back to an in breath or out breath and continue observing and making mental notes of those observations.

Jeffrey Schwartz is a neuropsychiatrist affiliated with UCLA and is the coauthor of several books, including You Are Not Your Brain, Brain Lock, *and* The Mind and the Brain.

LETTING GO

Bill Jensen

When it comes to relationships, my subtraction skills absolutely suck. It's an epic fail. The reason is simple: throughout my life I have tried to make too many relationships work long past their expiration dates.

As a boss, there have been several times when I should have let someone go long before he or she heard the umpteenth warning. I just couldn't. "There's so much potential here," I justified. There have been scores of creative partnerships, alliances, and projects that fell flat because I stayed with "Can't we work this out?" for far too long.

Loyalty is a most amazing quality. Except when it isn't.

During your career, you will have hundreds, perhaps thousands, of relationships. If you're lucky, most of them not only will help you get the job done, they also will enhance who you are as a person. You won't want to let them go. Even with that good luck, a few of them will still be stinkers. The stinkers are the ones that don't deserve you and what you have to offer.

The wisdom we all need is in a poem called "A Reason, a Season, and a Lifetime," attributed to Brian A. Chalker:

> People come into your life for a reason, a season, or a
> lifetime. When you figure out which it is, you know
> exactly what to do.

For the bosses and jobs that are stinkers or that provide only short-term value to you, don't whine and don't give less than your best. Do your best but figure out what lesson you were there to learn. There's always at least one. Learn it. Internalize it. Treasure it. Then thank those involved and *move on,* grateful for what you've learned.

For the bosses and jobs and teammates you would love to hang on to forever, realize that our role as humans is to grow. And growing usually means letting go of something that you've been holding on to for a while.

Letting go means creating room for new lessons, new opportunities. Whenever I let go—each and every time—I find that something or someone new and wonderful is waiting for me.

Bill Jensen (simplerwork.com) is author of Simplicity *and a coauthor of* Hacking Work.

THE PULSE OF LIFE

Tony Schwartz

For nearly a decade now, I've begun my workdays by focusing for 90 minutes, uninterrupted, on the task I decide the night before is the most important one I'll face the next day. After 90 minutes, I take a break.

To make this possible, I turn off my e-mail while I'm working, close all the windows on my computer, and let the phone go to voice mail if it rings. I typically get more work done during those 90 minutes and feel more satisfied with my output than I do for any comparable period of time the rest of the day. It can be tough on some days to fully focus for 90 minutes, but I always have a clear stopping time, which makes it easier.

I launched this practice because I long ago discovered that my energy, my will, and my capacity for intense focus diminish as the day wears on. Anything really challenging that I put off tends not to get done, and it's the most difficult work that tends to generate the greatest enduring value.

I first made this discovery while writing a book. At the time, I'd written three previous books. For each one, I'd dutifully sit down at my desk at 7 a.m., and I'd often stay there until 7 p.m. Looking back, I probably spent more time avoiding writing than I did actually writing. Instead, I spent an inordinate amount of time and energy making lists, responding to e-mail, answering the phone, and keeping my desk clean and my files incredibly well organized. There were days I never got to writing at all. It was incredibly frustrating.

At the heart of my work at The Energy Project is helping people and organizations build highly precise, deliberate practices done at specific times so that they eventually become automatic and don't require much expenditure of energy or self-discipline, akin to brushing your teeth at night.

It was this approach that I applied to the book I was writing and at other times to whatever I happened to be working on. The effect on my efficiency has been staggering. I wrote my fourth book in less than half the time I had invested in any of the three previous ones.

I don't get it right every day, but this single practice of working in 90-minute cycles—pulsing—has been life-changing for me. Try it for one week. Let me know what you discover.

I think you'll be amazed.

Tony Schwartz (tonyschwartz.com) is the president and CEO of The Energy Project (theenergy project.com) and the author of Be Excellent at Anything.

OBSERVATION ZEN

David Sherwin

I was traveling through central Japan on a brief sabbatical from my work as a designer. But being a designer is something that one cannot easily escape. Everywhere I go, I long to reshape what's around me into some new and improved—albeit imagined—form.

While riding the Tokyo subway, I could not stop myself from filling my notebook with ideas for all sorts of things that would help those sleepy-eyed salarymen, such as briefcases that doubled as pillows and fit perfectly into the seat gaps on the green JR Line and a series of vending machines that would sanitize and re-fill bottles with drinks commuters could carry and reuse on their daily commute, saving millions of plastic bottles and aluminum cans from being produced and recycled. Of course, I was not naive enough to believe that the latter innovation would be accepted without cultural friction.

Design is work. Thinking about design is work. Pondering what should be thought about in order to design is work. Back at home, while I was cutting vegetables for a stir-fry dinner, gears continued to whir in my mind regarding the problems my masters had set before me. It wasn't until I'd been meditating for some time that I understood on a fundamental level how work—and its analog design—is closely intertwined with thought and reflection.

As a designer, I have spent an increasing amount of time observing others. This includes my clients as they wrestle with difficult business problems; my subjects as I guide them through usability tests, empathizing with their frustration and delight; and my colleagues as they cast off failure after failure in search of the most elegant solution to a thorny design challenge.

Observation, however, is not work. It is direct experience, which does not necessarily require a critical eye to appreciate. "What can be met with recognition is not re-alization itself, because realization is not reached with a discriminating mind," the Zen master Dogen once wrote.

In our busy lives, it is often a struggle to tease out the act of observation from that of reflection (thinking and pondering). In practice, we routinely skip reflection to arrive at a design idea in one lightning-fast gesture. But the germ of the idea is always the ob-servation; that is what leads to genesis.

Glimmers of great ideas usually emerge from seeing the relationships between seemingly disparate things without distraction.

David Sherwin (changeorder.typepad.com) is the principal designer at frog design and the author of Creative Workshop *and* Success by Design. *He adapted this from his* Design Mind *article "Zen and the Art of Design."*

DO NOTHING

Jeff Unger

When I was a new lawyer, my boss and mentor (and later my friend) used to irritate me by giving me Yoda-like words of wisdom—some obvious, some not so much. Now, almost 20 years later, I realize how lucky I was to have had a mentor like him and how valuable his lessons were.

One of the most irritating bits of advice was "Sometimes the hardest thing to do is nothing at all."

The first time I heard that was in the middle of a late-night closing of a $50 million transaction. The lender imposed some last-minute conditions, which were frustrating to our client. The client wanted me to browbeat the lender into submission (as if a newly minted lawyer in San Diego could have that sort of impact on a career finance lawyer in Manhattan). I went into my boss's office for advice and help to work up my ire sufficiently to call the other lawyer. My mentor listened, reclined in his aged chair, and said, "Sometimes the hardest thing to do is nothing at all."

That's literally all he said. I left the office thinking, What the hell is he talking about?! I went home, my head spinning.

Well, the next morning, the lender had changed its position entirely. I had done nothing, and my client thought I was an amazing hotshot young lawyer. Over the next few years, that client and I developed a great friendship as I worked on about a billion dollars of transactions for him.

Did my mentor think through this strategically and know that the lender's attorney would have to change his position? I thought so.

Years later, I realized that he didn't have any special insight at all. There was no strategic thinking. There was no crystal ball. He had just learned over several decades as a lawyer that people sometimes change their minds and that although it was possible that I would have to eventually deal with the objectionable term, it was also possible that it might go away on its own. He simply had the maturity, experience, and wisdom I didn't at the time.

More than 20 years later, I realize that the best legal tactic is frequently doing absolutely nothing. Too frequently, lawyers are ready to charge, pick up the phone, fire off an e-mail or a letter, and forget that doing absolutely nothing might be a viable tactic to consider.

Simple advice but never easy to hear or take.

Jeffrey Unger is the founder of eMinutes.com, a law practice with the simple mission of being the world's best option for forming and maintaining small businesses.

A QUIET MIND

Kevin Meyer

I'm one of those folks who can't resist an idea, and I get a lot of them. I simply don't understand the concept of boredom. For years I'd chase every idea to see where it might lead. Before long I was juggling dozens of them.

Throw in my job of running a company and a chaotic family medical situation that prevents planning more than a week in advance and you've got a recipe for some sort of breakdown.

I was on the verge of one of those a few years back, so I did something a bit radical: I hopped a plane to Hawaii for three days, leaving everyone and everything behind. I figured a couple of days of wind and waves and sun could rebalance the soul. My wife supported my decision.

On that first escape I spent time catching up on projects, working on my laptop by the pool until the battery died and then sitting on the beach while it charged. Evening was more of the same. Catching up created temporary space, peace, and balance.

I began escaping to Hawaii about every four months, always at the last minute, when I knew the family medical situation was temporarily stable. Although the first trip focused on catching up, later trips became more about personal meditation and reflection.

What I realized over time was that the time-outs helped remove the distraction and replace it with focus. I relished the break from the routine, being accountable only to myself, the quietude, and solitude. Being close to nature calmed the senses and quieted the mind.

Once I realized that I was becoming more effective by removing distraction, I began to apply that concept every day. I have the most beautiful commute in the world: a few miles up the scenic Pacific Coast Highway and then down a windy empty road through vineyards and avocado fields. In the past I would crank the music or listen to news. Now I commute in silence, allowing my thoughts and ideas to develop, prioritize, and settle. On the commute into work I plan the day, especially the two or three key tasks that must get done. On the commute home I reflect on how the day went and how it could have been improved.

Taking a break helps promote mindfulness. That mindfulness helps organize and prioritize thoughts and projects, leading to less juggling. Less juggling promotes peace and balance and thus effectiveness.

Kevin Meyer (kevinmeyer.com) is the former president of a medical device manufacturer and the author of Beachfront Leading.

UNSELLING

Jonathan Kay

 I've always liked talking. I'm good at it. So when I started in business, I figured I'd go into sales, get people to listen to me talk, and get them to buy stuff. But it was the worst. Selling required me to completely remove myself from the picture. The company I worked for didn't want me to be myself. They had a formula, and if you followed it, you got the results they wanted.

I literally stopped selling and left the company. As my business life went on, I vowed I wouldn't ever sell. But I kept talking, helping create "buzz" for companies, and got a reputation for promoting people and businesses without selling.

A woman organizing a big conference reached out to me to be a speaker. When she asked me how much I charged for speaking, I thought, I don't ever charge for speaking. I think when someone pays you to speak, you can't be totally you and say exactly what you want; you have to say something they want to hear. When you speak for free, you're free of that; you're doing it because you love the content. I do, anyway.

But I needed the money for a new business I was starting. So I wrote an e-mail to her saying I didn't charge for speaking, I loved to talk about creating buzz, and I wouldn't even feel genuine about it anymore because I was being paid.

Her response was, "Oh, my gosh, how are you this honest? I'm going to make sure no matter what that you get paid!" I had to laugh. I hadn't sold; I had told the unvarnished truth.

It was the opposite of selling, and I ended up getting the money anyway. And that's been my whole approach to business: figuring out how can I do something for someone with no sales implication and truly believe something good will happen.

Sometimes when you hope but don't ask for something, that something comes to you simply because you believe in what you're doing.

And I've learned the right way, a constructive way, to remove myself from the picture. I've learned to listen, stand outside myself to listen, truly listen, to feedback, to criticism, without having a comeback or a preconceived notion of a response. If you're formulating a response while someone's telling you something, you can't be objective.

Yin and yang, right? All very Zen: removing the ask and making sure the real me is in the picture while making sure I'm not in the picture so I can listen and learn on the other.

Jonathan Kay is the founder and chief operating officer of Apptopia.com, a marketplace designed to help broker the sale of mobile apps.

STAY OUT OF YOUR WAY

pleasefindthis

The Leftovers

*I made myself from all the love you
no longer wanted.*

One of the first things you're taught in design school, if it's at all halfway decent, is that you should take away absolutely everything you do not need. That's what's meant by the phrase "form follows function"; it means don't design or create things to look pretty or add things that don't need to be there.

Things look beautiful and have a natural emotional ergonomic when you strip them to their core and only their essence remains. When things become too complicated, you lose your audience. You might ask, but what about Jackson Pollock? His paintings are incredibly complex. Yes, there is nothing else *but* the idea of complexity in his paintings.

My best-known online artwork, *I Wrote This for You*—a collaborative, international, minimal, anonymous prose and photography project that became a popular book—has no name on it or any other traditional identity features in it, yet thousands of people relate to it every day. (It doesn't even have a copyright symbol.)

They step into the picture to fill the space I've left by stepping out of it. They step into the frame in an intensely personal way that only they could, given their individuality.

If it has taught me anything, it's that if you can find something you're good at and you can be focused enough to remove all the distractions around it, including your ego, you will shine. And people will be attracted to that kind of light.

Stay out of the way of whatever you're trying to accomplish.

pleasefindthis (iwrotethisforyou.me) is an award-winning new media artist and the bestselling author of I Wrote This for You, *based in South Africa.*

CODA

On the evening of February 26, 2012, the motion picture *The Artist* won the Oscar hat trick—best picture, best actor in a leading role, and best direction—at the eighty-fourth Academy Awards, beating out the biggest names in Hollywood. Although it had garnered 10 nominations, *The Artist* was a dark horse in the race for the Oscars as a French film with a director and cast virtually unknown to the American audience. What made *The Artist* such an underdog was that it was shot in the style of the motion pictures of the 1920s: black and white and silent (except, of course, for music).

It was also a study in subtraction.

I watched it with my wife in the comfort of our living room two weeks before the awards (courtesy of a friend in the academy). I'd been wanting to see it for months simply because of its subtractive nature. Who makes a silent black-and-white film in the age of everything 3-D?

The Artist did not disappoint me, and it was a master class in the art of subtraction at its finest. Every law of subtraction was employed to produce a story experience every bit as compelling and powerful as, say, James Cameron's technical wizardry in the 3-D movie *Avatar*.

I realized as we watched it that I'd never seen my wife so emotionally engaged in a movie before. I watched her as much as I watched the movie. The only explanation for that is subtraction.

The story didn't just happen on the screen. It also happened in our minds. And the emotions were intensified because we had to supply the missing information, inject ourselves and our feelings and our words into the story. Some of the most powerful moments in film are those without words. The two-minute-long silent scene in Mike Nichols's 1967 classic *The Graduate* that film critic Joe Morgenstern called one the most indelible and ingenious in cinema history comes to mind as an example. It's the one in which Dustin Hoffman's character of young college graduate Benjamin Braddock plunges into the swimming pool clad in full scuba gear, spear gun and all, and remains submerged at the bottom, contemplating his so-called life, while all the audience gets is a close-up of the character and the sound of him breathing. Because of what came before in the film, we as viewers have all the context needed to interpret what the character is thinking and feeling. At the same time, the scene remains open to interpretation, and we're allowed to inject our personal experiences and emotions into it.

The Artist was two hours' worth of those moments.

The story in *The Artist* is one of fame and diminishing fame. It's Hollywood, 1927, and silent movie star George Valentin wonders if the arrival of talking pictures will cause him to fade into oblivion. Of course it does, but not before he sparks with Peppy Miller, a young dancer set for a big break, which she gets thanks to George. As the movie studio goes with talkies and abandons silent movies, George's star fades. "No one wants to hear you talk, George," according to the studio head. Peppy becomes a big star amid the backdrop of the 1929 stock market crash. By 1932, George is in ruins; Peppy is a big celebrity. It is, of course, a love story, with Peppy having never lost the original spark.

But all along, I wondered, as I'm sure everyone watching did: Why can't George simply talk in the movies? All along we think that it's all simply a matter of stubborn pride. But, I thought, that cannot be all of it. And it can't be just, as the story suggests, that people want "fresh meat."

We do not find out until the very end, when he utters just two words, which explain the entire plot. George's words are not important. It's how he says them: with a thick French accent. We realize in that moment why no one in America wants to hear him talk.

I'm not sure I've ever been so satisfied with an ending. As a matter of fact, I'm usually dissatisfied with movie plots and endings because they are simplistic and predictable.

The Artist is a brilliant and beautiful display of the laws of subtraction and how they can help you win in the age of excess everything.

NOTES, SOURCES, AND FURTHER READINGS

A complete list of sources, links, permissions, and references may be found by visiting LawsofSubtraction.com.

For those interested in further developing their subtractive abilities, I've created a self-driven playbook called *Box of Less*. It contains activities, exercises, video links, and reading material for each of the six laws of subtraction.

It too is available at LawsofSubtraction.com.

INDEX